Strumming
the Guitar

Guitar Strumming for Beginners and Upward with Audio and Video

By Gareth Evans

ISBN   978-1-912135-55-4

Written by Gareth Evans

Copyright © 2019 by Intuition Publications

www.guitar-book.com

Introduction

Welcome to Strumming for Guitar. A guide, solely on the subject of strumming the guitar taking you from the ground up for beginners and towards intermediate level.

The book has an incremental, detailed and methodical approach allowing the beginner to absorb everything important from the start. While not going too fast for a slower learner there is plenty of material to occupy a faster learner who will find challenges they'll need to spend time on. The book contains 70 strumming patterns in total, all shown with easy-to-understand diagrams.

As the general difficulty level progresses, separate approaches are taken on strumming alone, changing chords alone and coordinating chord changes while strumming, therefore encouraging a thorough approach throughout with components broken down at every level. Reading rhythmical notation is covered and further details, nuances and tips are given and assisted with professionally hand drawn illustrations as the book progresses.

Each section concludes with a musical study piece using the skills learnt and practised. Exercises and musical study pieces are demonstrated with audio. For some parts, videos (21) are used, where it serves to make for a better explanation. The symbol for audio looks like this: 🔊)) and the symbol for video looks like this: ▶

Make sure your guitar is tuned to standard tuning EADGBE. A guide to tuning a guitar can be found on www.guitar-book.com/how-to-tune-a-guitar or just go to guitar-book.com > Lessons & Tips > How to Tune a Guitar.

The link to the Audio and Video
files can be found on page 90.

Contents

Chapter 5 - Fretting Finger Independence

Chapter 6 - Chord Changes on 8th Notes (Part 2)

How to Read Chord Diagrams

First a quick primer on how to read chord diagrams. Chord diagrams provide a graphical representation of the fret-board. In the following example the parts and their functions are labeled.

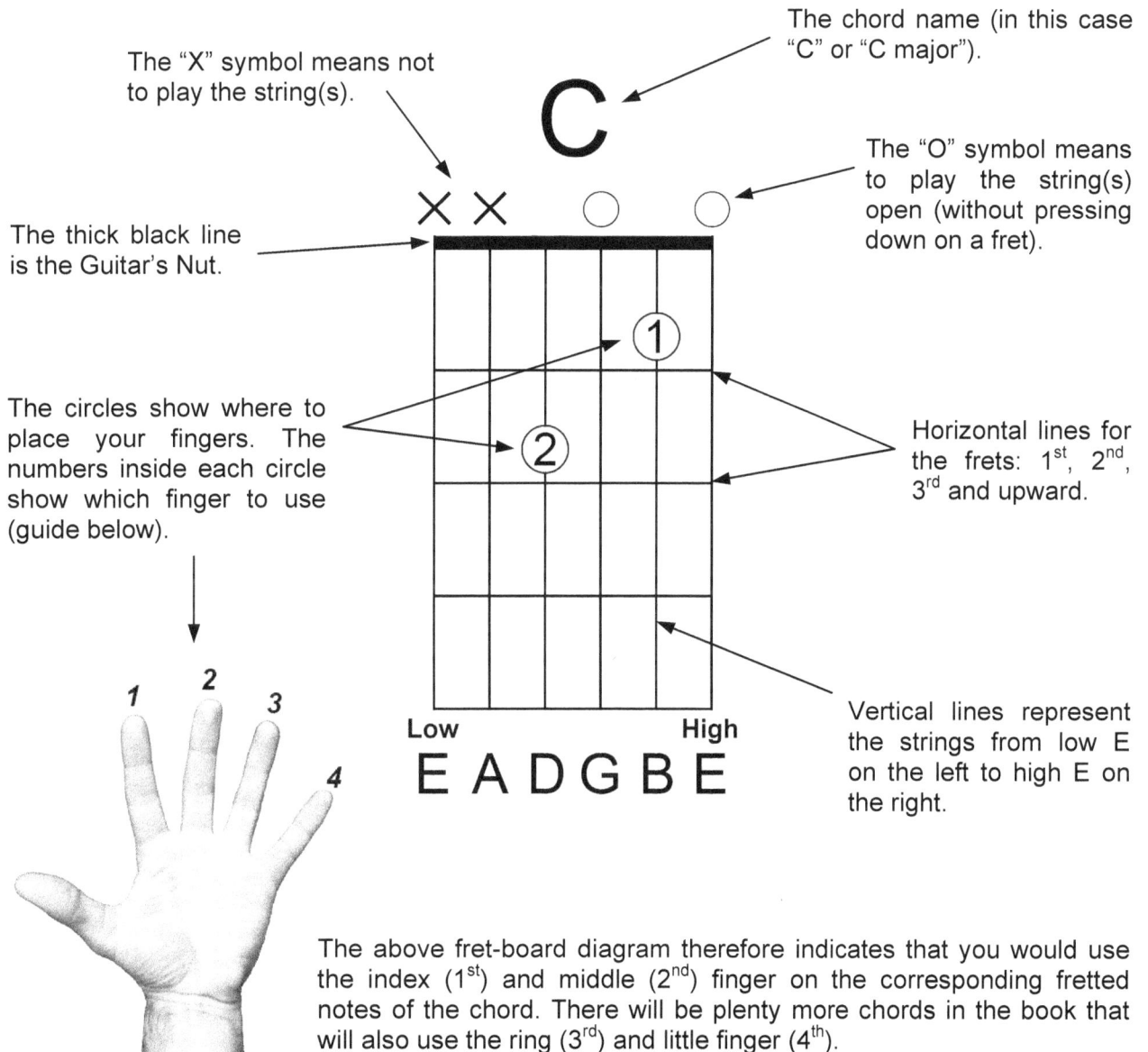

The chord name (in this case "C" or "C major").

The "X" symbol means not to play the string(s).

The "O" symbol means to play the string(s) open (without pressing down on a fret).

The thick black line is the Guitar's Nut.

The circles show where to place your fingers. The numbers inside each circle show which finger to use (guide below).

Horizontal lines for the frets: 1st, 2nd, 3rd and upward.

Low　High
E A D G B E

Vertical lines represent the strings from low E on the left to high E on the right.

The above fret-board diagram therefore indicates that you would use the index (1st) and middle (2nd) finger on the corresponding fretted notes of the chord. There will be plenty more chords in the book that will also use the ring (3rd) and little finger (4th).

The Strumming Hand

Let's look at how to hold a plectrum. The way we hold a plectrum for strumming is very similar to how we would hold it for playing single note melodies (e.g. for a guitar solo). Curl the index finger around and place the plectrum between the side of this finger and the pad of the thumb. The plectrum should point in more or less the same direction that the palm faces.

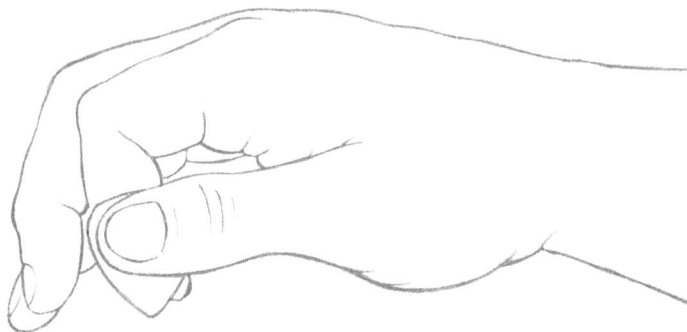

If new to strumming, you may feel like pushing the rest of the fingers together, almost like a fist, to get more control and hold everything in place, as shown in the picture to the right. This can make the hand a little too rigid for the fluid movements needed for strumming.

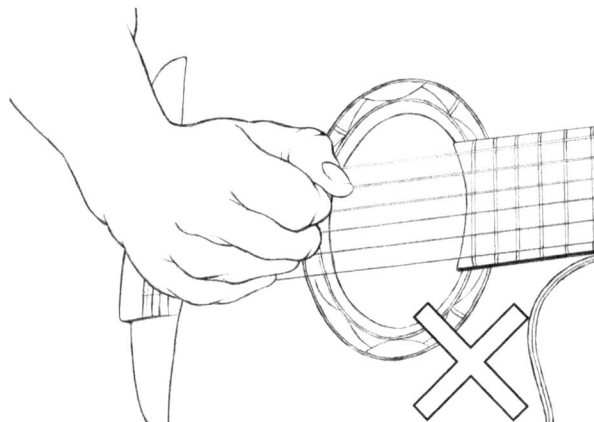

With the other fingers *not* pushed together, even if they are still close to each other, strumming becomes easier, as shown in the picture below left. Another variation is with fingers spread out more, as shown below right. Either of these two postures, or anywhere between them, will work best to allow the strumming hand freedom to move fluidly.

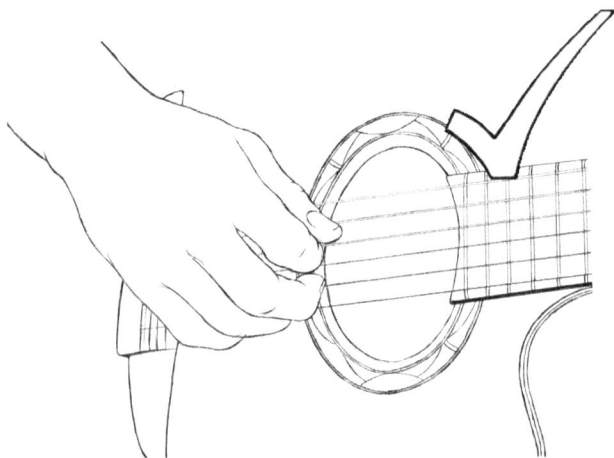

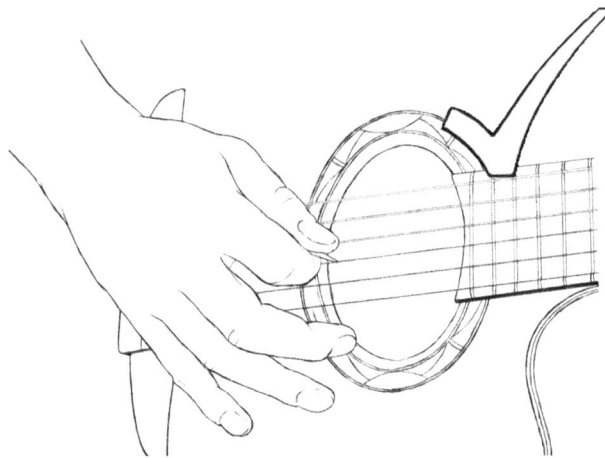

Let's start off by strumming down and up across all six open strings. "Open" means the strings are played with no frets pushed down. The plectrum should move in an arc of motion as shown in the picture to the right. As we strum it's not just the forearm that moves down and up, the wrist should rotate your hand a little also.

If you already know any chords you could use one. One that uses all six strings will be easier as you won't have to avoid any strings. If not, open strings will do, chords will be introduced soon.

You may have found that straight forward and are producing clean sounding strums like on the video. If not, looking at strumming technique in more detail, as we are about to, may help.

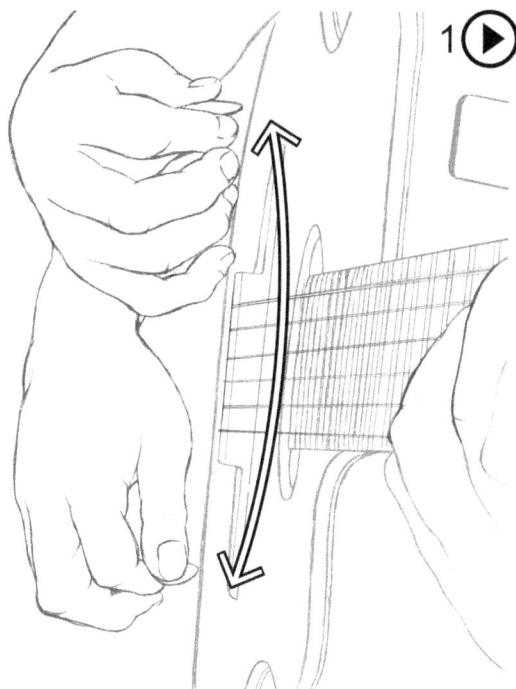

1 ▶

Where Along the Strings Should I Strum?

The strings have different resistance depending on how far along them you play. For a beginner the differences can be more noticeable.

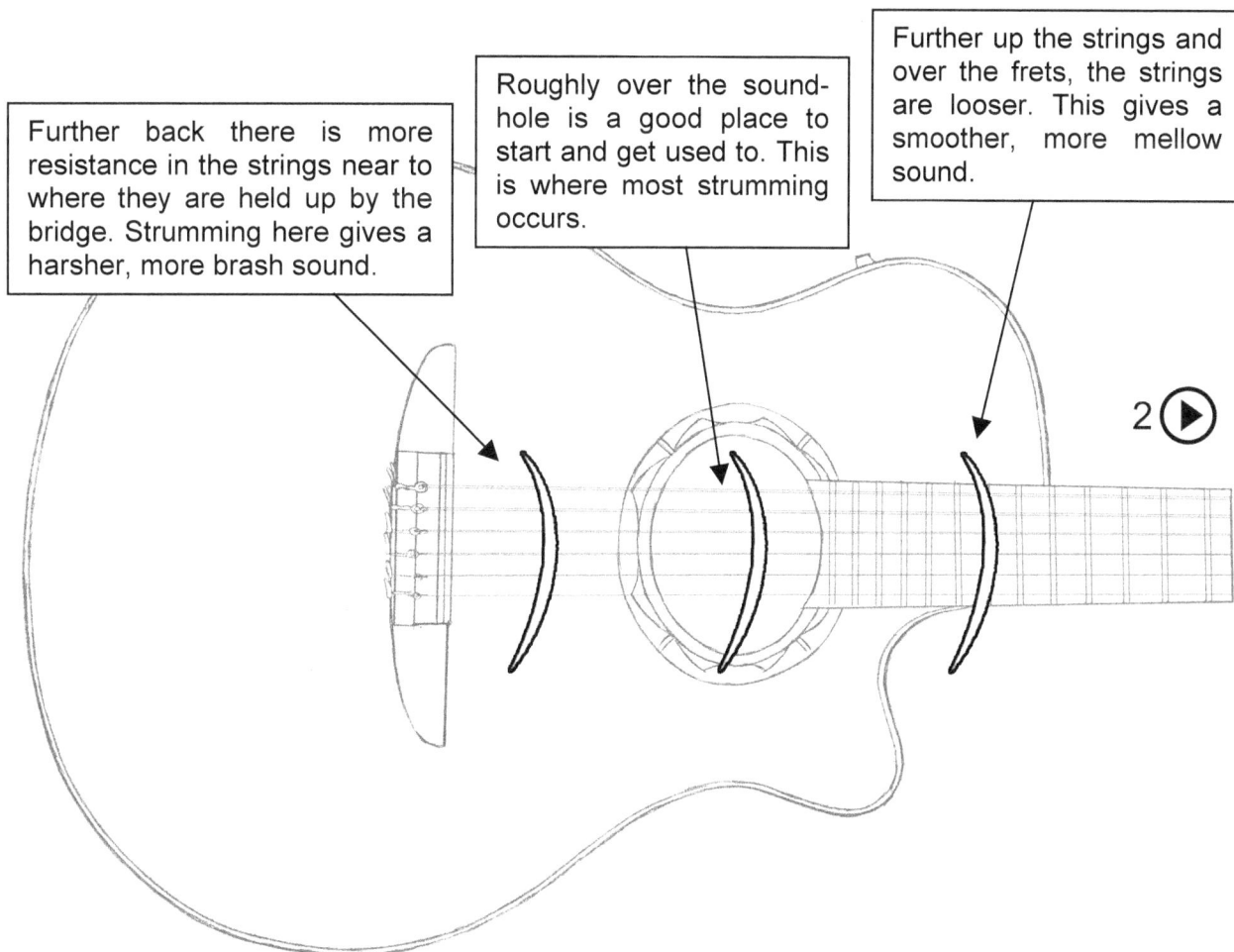

Further back there is more resistance in the strings near to where they are held up by the bridge. Strumming here gives a harsher, more brash sound.

Roughly over the sound-hole is a good place to start and get used to. This is where most strumming occurs.

Further up the strings and over the frets, the strings are looser. This gives a smoother, more mellow sound.

2 ▶

How Tightly Should I Hold the Plectrum?

We need to hold the plectrum firmly enough so that it stays correctly within our grip but not too firmly, otherwise the plectrum won't pass smoothly over the strings as we strum. The following pictures give an idea (and would also be exemplified on previous video 1).

Downward Strum

Upward Strum

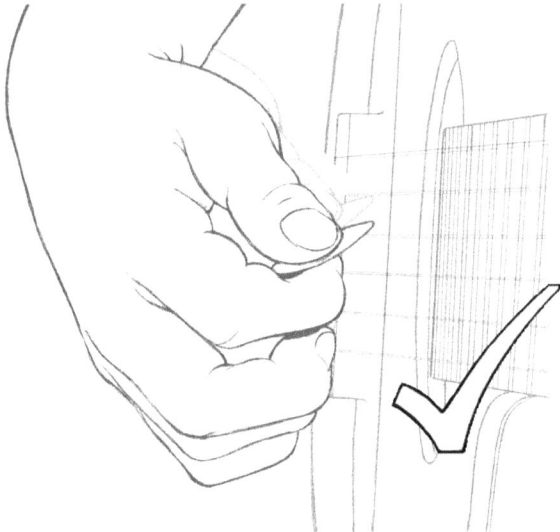
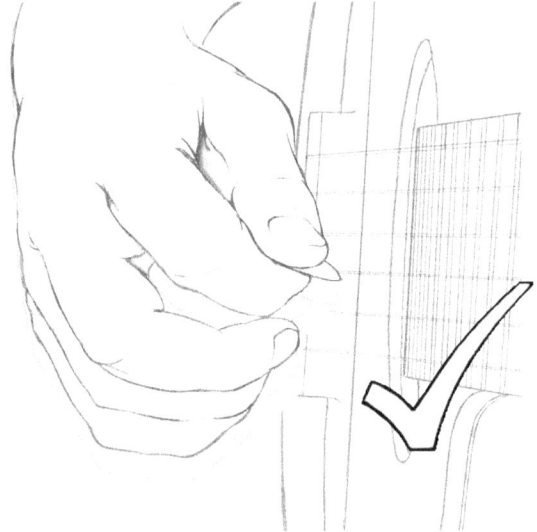

An issue for beginners can be that we hold the plectrum too rigidly. Often, the reason for this is a feeling that if we don't hold the plectrum firmly enough it will slip within our grip. This can result in a harsher sound with the plectrum pushing into the strings, sometimes with the plectrum even getting momentarily stuck. The two pictures below show this; the hand is rigid and the tightly held plectrum is forcing through the strings on the way down and up, as also demonstrated on the video.

3 ▶

Downward Strum

Upward Strum

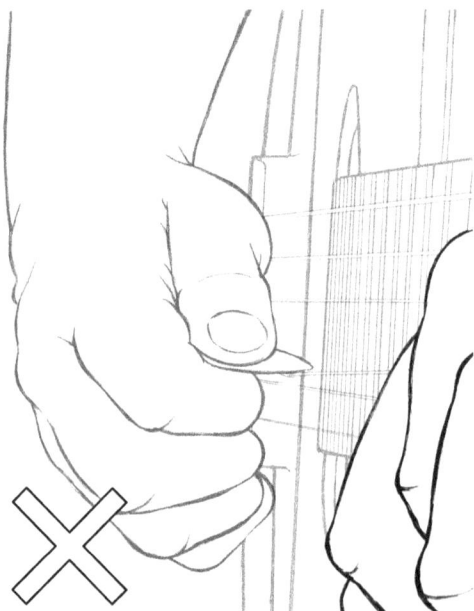
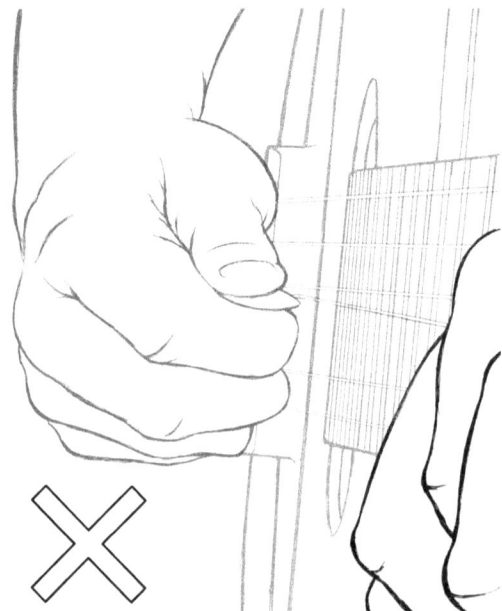

If we hold the plectrum without such a tight grip, strumming can become easier, but in doing so, we may find that after a few strums the plectrum has moved or rotated within our grip. In the picture below, the plectrum has slipped and is no longer pointing in the same direction as the palm faces.

While teaching I have noticed some beginners occasionally pause for a moment and use their other hand to reposition the plectrum before recommencing strumming. It may take some practise at first to get the balance right between making sure the plectrum stays in place and strumming fluidly. There is a little more specific detail on this in the following part called "The Fine Detail".

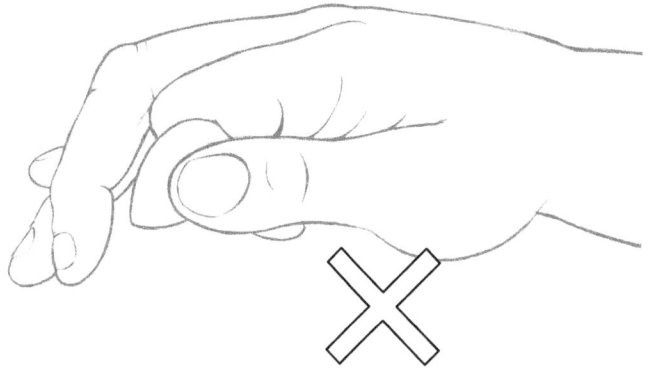

Tip: A thinner plectrum can make strumming easier for beginners. A thinner plectrum is more forgiving as it gives way, bending slightly to compensate for a lack of fluidity in the hand. A plectrum at a width of .60mm or below can help if you find initial difficulty with a thicker plectrum. This is particularly true for upward strums; for instance, if you tend to push the plectrum into the strings on the upward strums, a softer pick of .60mm or less will bend to make up for it.

The Fine Detail

Experienced strummers may not be aware of this, but when strumming, the grip used on the plectrum is not constant it actually changes subtly (this is somewhat different to how we would grip a plectrum while playing single note melodies).

On Downward strums the thumb is pushing the plectrum down with greater force, while the index finger applies only enough pressure to hold the plectrum in place within your grip.

On Upward strums the index finger is pushing the plectrum up with greater force, while the thumb applies only enough pressure to hold the plectrum in place within your grip.

At the point between either of the aforementioned downward or upward strums, the thumb and index finger are applying similar force to each other before changing over.

Players who are new to strumming may lack control of these subtleties. This is something that comes with practise. It's like walking, our brain controls many different muscles in a specific sequence in order to walk, but we are not consciously aware of which muscles and in what sequence, it's just something we learned to do with experience. Whether you choose to consciously apply this subtle factor to strumming, or absorb it over the course of experience (like many of the experienced strummers would have as mentioned) it is interesting to know.

Upward Strums

Why do upwards strums seem more awkward to play at first? To many, strumming upward is often trickier and feels less natural than downward strumming. This is likely due to how we are used to moving the hand in the direction of the little finger (like a downward strum) when making brisk arm movements that require accuracy. Some examples would be using a hammer on a nail, playing darts, casting a fishing rod or playing the drums.

Brisk movements requiring accuracy, where the hand goes primarily in the direction of the thumb may exist but are not as common. This is why strumming upward can take a bit more getting use to at first. The more you do it the better you'll get.

Avoiding Strings

There are chords in which certain strings are to be avoided while strumming. For example, the D major open chord shown below. The term "*open chord*" means a chord in which there is at least one open string. For this chord only the D, G, B and high E strings are to be strummed, with the A and low E strings to be avoided.

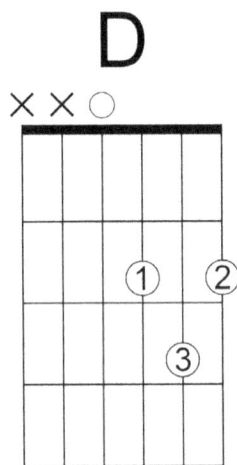

Rather than try to accurately and specifically hit the D string at the start of downward strums and leave it after upwards strums, it is easier to change the angle of our strum and use a tighter arc of motion, as the below picture shows, when compared to the larger arc of motion shown at the top of page 7.

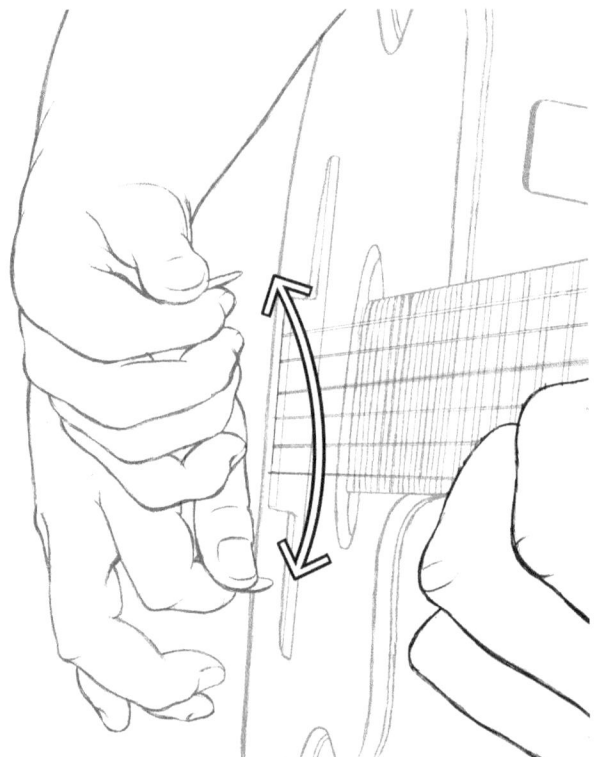

You might miss the D string occasionally (either at the start of downward strums or at the end of upwards strums) but this isn't a huge problem because the G, B and high E strings still contain the intervals (notes) that comprise a D major chord. It is better to avoid hitting the A and low E strings as these are not in the D major chord (especially not the low E string).

It is worth practising strumming like this to improve your skill of missing strings. Another chord that can be used would be an A major open chord, for which the low E string is to be avoided. There are many chords in which strings are to be avoided. Apply the same above technique when strumming them.

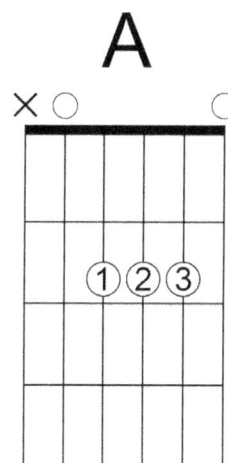

Finger-style Players

Finally, if you are a finger-style player, strum by holding the fingers as though you are gripping a plectrum. Use the nail of the index finger for downward strums and the nail of the thumb for upward strums.

5 ▶

All of the former advice applies to the finger style way of strumming, apart from of course "How to hold a plectrum" and "How Tightly Should we Hold the Plectrum?". The part titled "The Fine detail" applies too, albeit minus the plectrum.

The Basics of Rhythm

When strumming rhythms, the hand should move consistently with the beat, meaning that the strumming hand should keep moving down and up, including in-between the actual strums. This consistent down and up down movement is a bit like a car engine running, with the actual strums being when it's in gear. This helps us to keep time, as well as be aware of the space between strums, making it easier to come in at the right place when we do strum.

The term for the strumming movements when there is no contact with strings is "*ghost strums*". We will start off with a short rhythm that uses all ghost strums in order to get the underlying movement needed before we start actually strumming. Count out loud the following while ghost strumming down and up, as shown in the pictures. The "+" when referred to verbally, should be said as the word "*and*" so you would repeat "*one and two and one and two and*" etc.

6 ▶

| 1 | + | 2 | + |

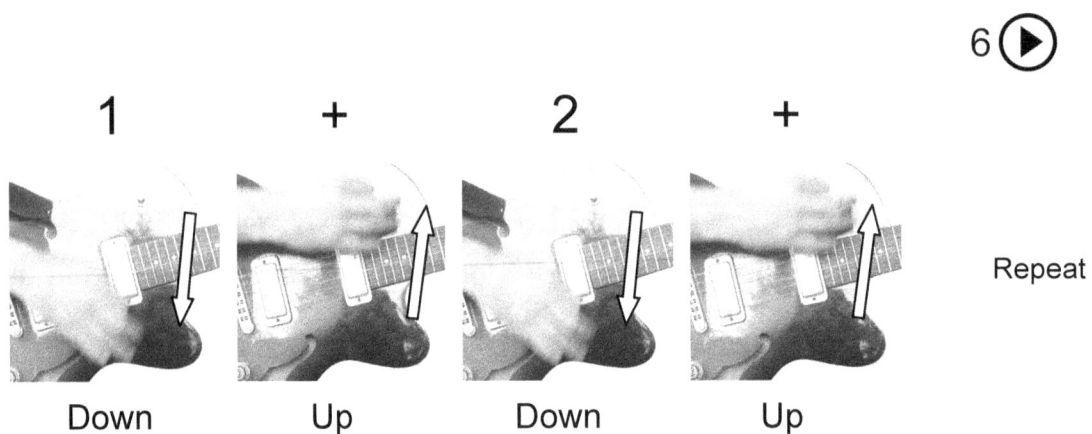

| Down | Up | Down | Up |

Repeat

Soon, we will introduce actual strums to the pattern while using a chord. One that uses all six strings will be easier for your strumming hand at first as we won't have to focus on avoiding certain strings. Here are a few chords to choose from, with easiest for the fretting hand on the left, getting more difficult for the fretting hand to the right. Their full, unabbreviated, names are also given underneath each.

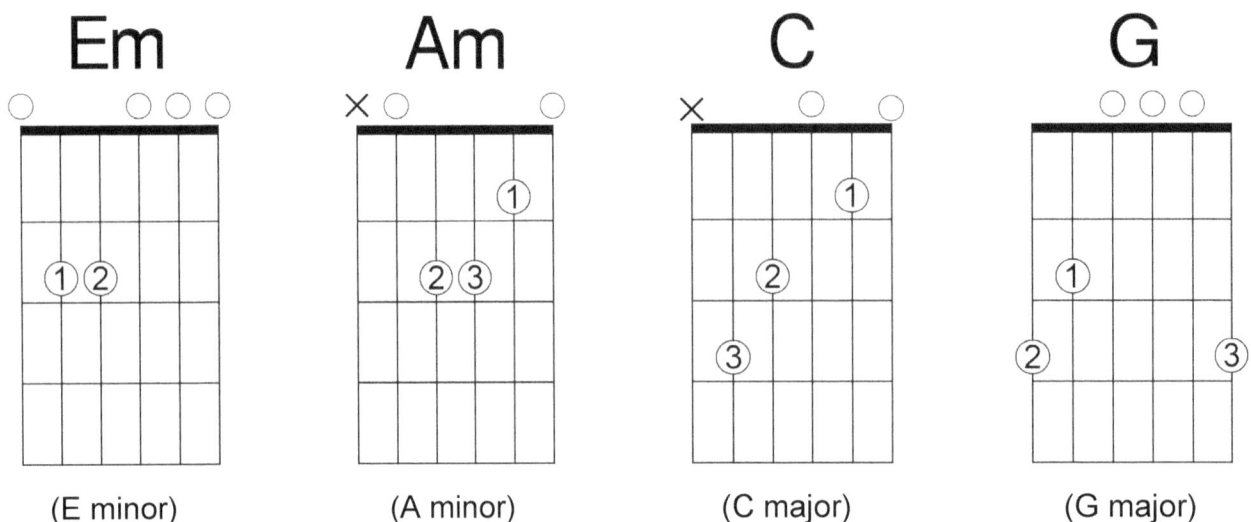

| Em | Am | C | G |
| (E minor) | (A minor) | (C major) | (G major) |

Simple Strumming Patterns

From hereon we will use arrow diagrams to represent the down and up movements of strumming. Large dark arrows indicate when to strum down or up while the smaller white arrows indicate ghost strums down or up. The first three exercises start by strumming on the stronger, numbered beats. The beats we would usually tap our foot too.

7 ▶

On Beat 1 only

On Beat 2 only

On Beats 1 and 2

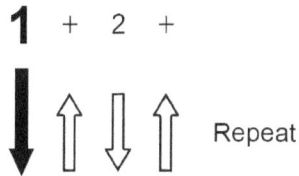

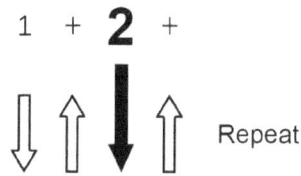

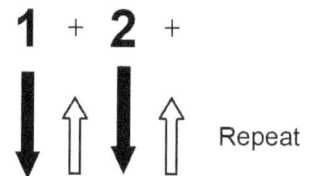

All of the video demonstrations for this section are at a tempo of 50bpm (50 beats per minute). Try these exercises on your own too while counting for yourself, or if it helps use the counting audio tracks 1+2+ to play over at various speeds. Simple eh? Great! Now for the *off-beats*. Off beats are in-between the stronger beats and can be harder to get used to at first because they are not usually as strongly ingrained into our natural sense of rhythm as much as the stronger beats are.

8 ▶

The First Off-beat

The Last Offbeat

Both Off-beats

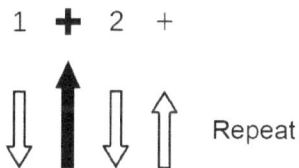

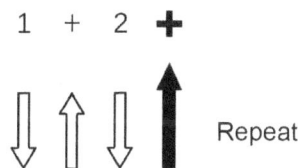

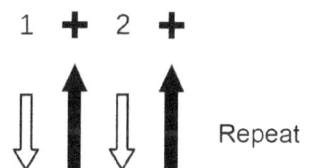

Once you've got the hang of those you should be able to get through the following ones on your own while counting for yourself or using the counting audio tracks 1+2+.

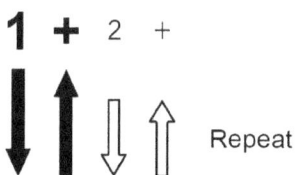

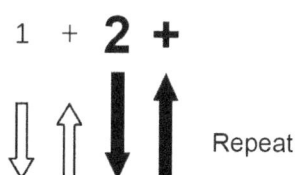

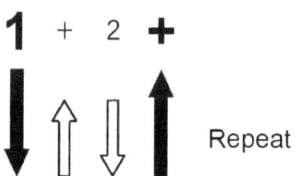

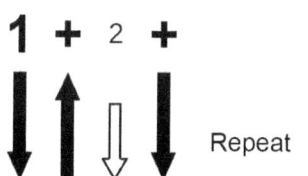

Reading Rhythmic Notation

The previous arrow diagrams are specific to guitar strumming. However, it can also be beneficial to understand the common language of music. From hereon rhythmic notation will also be included underneath all strumming patterns. Below is what rhythmic notation would look like with one of the previous exercises. A time signature, which will also be explained, is labelled too.

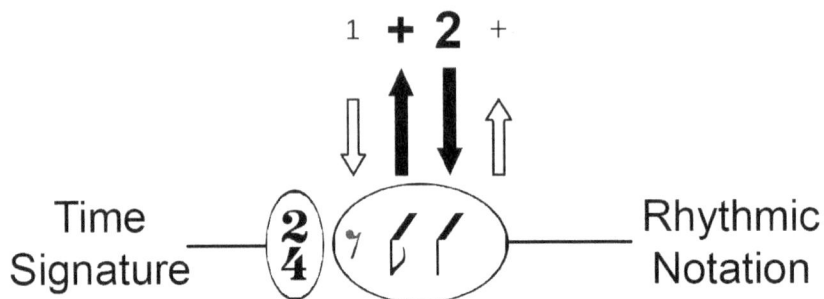

Rhythmic notation is used for when there is only the need to show the rhythm of the music, rather than indicating different note pitches as well (such as G, C#, A, E♭ etc.) Rhythmic notation looks a little different from standard notation in that it uses straight edged note symbols rather than curved edged ones. Below, each rhythmic notation symbol is shown as a counterpart, to the right of its standard notation symbol. Their fractional names are given above, while their equivalent classical terms have been written underneath.

Whole Note	**Half Note**	**Quarter Note**	**Eighth Note**
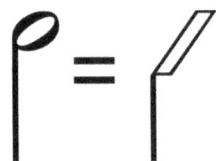		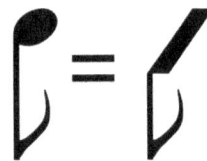	
(Semibreve)	(Minim)	(Crotchet)	(Quaver)

The note's stem is the straight line that comes from its head. For the above notes that have stems, the stem goes below the note's head. At other times the note's stem goes above, as shown in the example to the to the right with a quarter note.

The reason for any stem's direction, be that up or down, is simply tidiness within written music. For example, if an upward stem would clash with something else in the written music then it can be made a downward stem instead and vice versa. In this book the stems of the rhythmic notation will go downwards so that the heads of the notes are closer to the strumming arrow directions, as the example to the right shows.

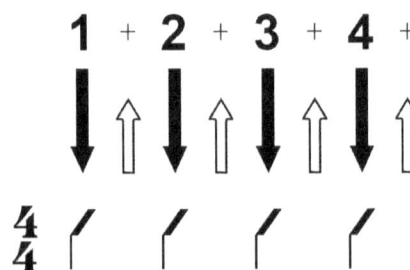

14

Below, is a chart showing the rhythmic notation symbols relative to each other. Fraction symbols have been added to the note's boxes because it works just the same as fractions, in fact you could say this is the musical version of fractions. Across the bottom of the chart, rhythm counting numbers (1 + 2 + 3 + 4 +) have also been added to show how this translates to how we would count rhythms.

We can use the vertical dividing lines in the chart to help us see how long any type of note lasts in comparison to another. For example, two quarter notes last the same amount of time as one half note. One quarter note lasts the same amount of time as two eighth notes etc.

The above chart shows how eighth notes look individually (like a quarter note with a tail coming from its stem). However, in a piece of music, when there is more than one eighth note in a row, often their stems are joined together, as shown below.

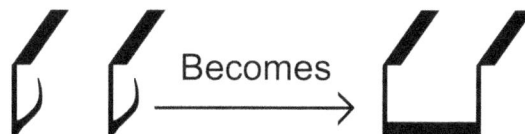

The most likely reason for this is because some time ago all music was written note for note by hand with a pen or pencil onto paper so it would have been a much more laborious process than using a computer. A line of eighth notes would have required each of their tails to be drawn from each of their stems, so instead, representing sequential eighth notes by simply drawing a line between their stems would have saved composers a lot of time.

Rests

There are also rests, which indicate when not to play. The aforementioned note values all have equivalent rests. Below is a chart. When used for rhythmic notation rests use the same symbols as they would for conventional notation.

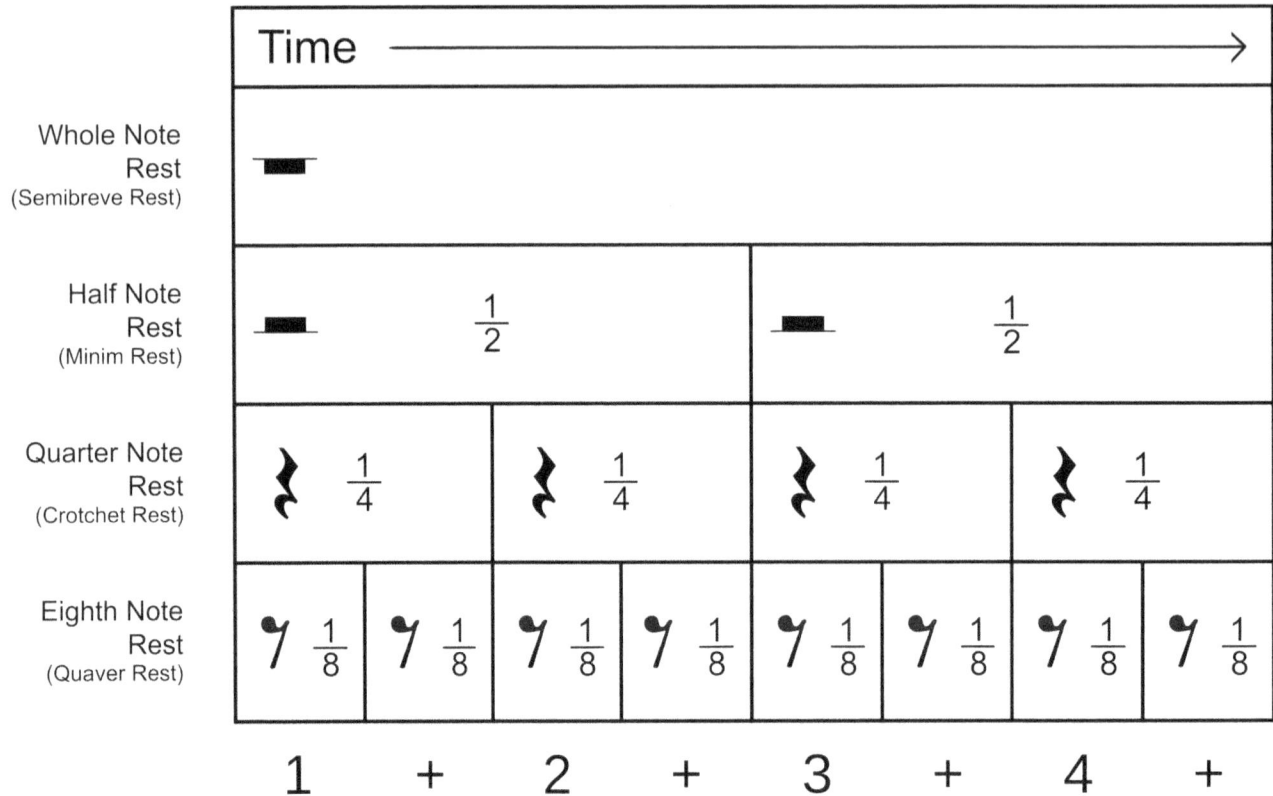

Time →							
Whole Note Rest (Semibreve Rest)							
Half Note Rest (Minim Rest)	$\frac{1}{2}$				$\frac{1}{2}$		
Quarter Note Rest (Crotchet Rest)	$\frac{1}{4}$		$\frac{1}{4}$		$\frac{1}{4}$		$\frac{1}{4}$
Eighth Note Rest (Quaver Rest)	$\frac{1}{8}$	$\frac{1}{8}$	$\frac{1}{8}$	$\frac{1}{8}$	$\frac{1}{8}$	$\frac{1}{8}$	$\frac{1}{8}$ $\frac{1}{8}$
	1	+	2	+	3	+	4 +

Note: Although whole note rests and half note rests will not be used in this book, they are included on the diagram for completeness and to put the rests that *will* be used into fuller context.

A dot after a note, or rest, increases its duration by a half of itself. Therefore, knowing that half of a quarter note is an eighth note, a dotted quarter note will last for an extra eighth note longer. Likewise, the same is true for a dotted quarter note rest. See diagrams below.

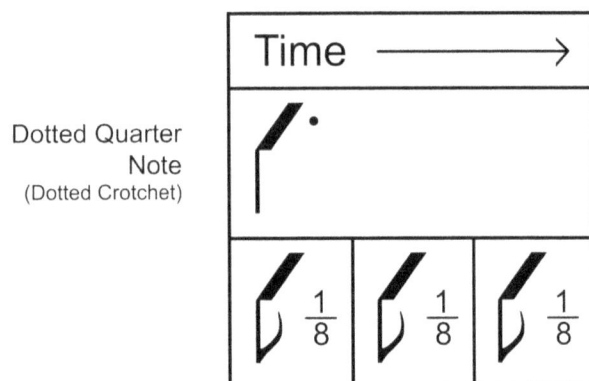

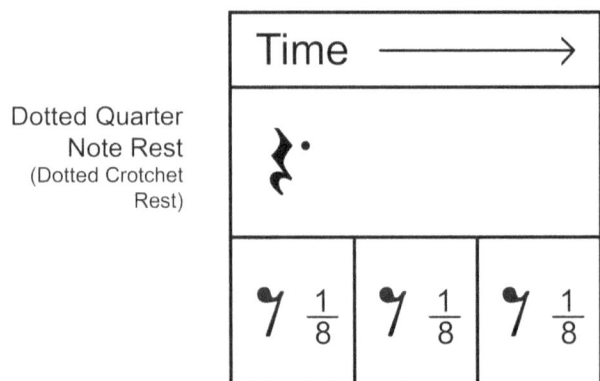

Dotted Quarter Note (Dotted Crotchet)

Time →		
$\frac{1}{8}$	$\frac{1}{8}$	$\frac{1}{8}$

Dotted Quarter Note Rest (Dotted Crotchet Rest)

Time →		
$\frac{1}{8}$	$\frac{1}{8}$	$\frac{1}{8}$

Ties

Ties fulfil a similar function to the dot, in that a tie increases the duration of a note. However with ties it is not an increase by a specific amount, but instead, by whichever note the first one is tied to, as the following examples show. Below is a quarter note, which is tied to an eighth note, making it last an extra eighth note longer.

Below is a whole note tied to another whole note making it last twice as long.

Both the above examples are taken from the strumming exercises and study pieces used later on in the book.

Time Signatures

Now that we have looked at the note and rest values, which will be used throughout the book, we'll have a look at basic time signatures. Music is organised into equal measures called bars. The length of the bars, are determined by what note value is considered as a beat and how many of these beats there are per bar. A time signature indicates this with two numbers, one on top of the other. The top number tells us how many beats there are per bar, while the bottom number tells us what note value is considered as a beat. Below are two examples.

The time signature to the right means two quarter note beats per bar (this time signature was shown at the beginning of this chapter underneath the exampled strumming pattern on page 14).

2/4

The next time signature shown to the right, is four quarter note beats per bar. Normally with fractions, you would write this as "one whole" and the previous time signature as "one half" but because we are distinguishing the beats, we write them as two quarters and four quarters.

4/4

There are other time signatures, but the above 4/4 is undoubtedly the most common time signature used in contemporary popular music. This time signature will be used throughout this book as we study strumming and chord changes.

Strumming Patterns A

Strumming Patterns in 4/4 Time

Let's try some strumming patterns within four quarter note beats per bar. Use a chord of your choice (Em, Am, C or G from page 12 would do). As these are the first patterns in 4/4 time there's a video of the first four at a tempo of 60bpm (60 beats per minute). These patterns can be played with counting audio tracks 1+2+3+4+ at various speeds, or while counting for your self, or with a metronome.

9 ▶

A1.

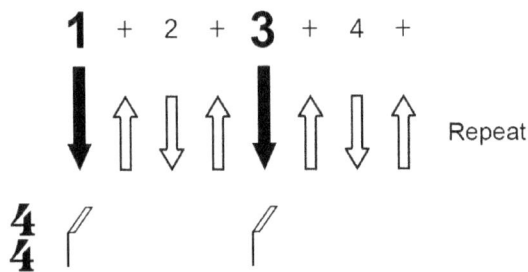

A2.

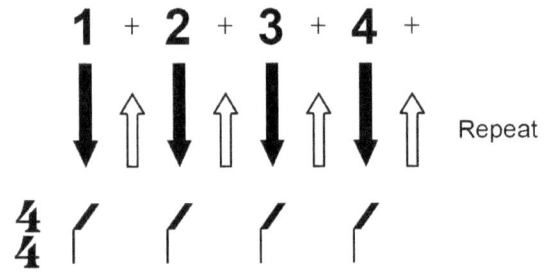

Now for some with a **+** in the strumming pattern.

A3.

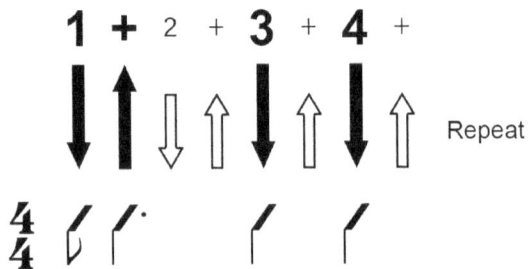

A4.

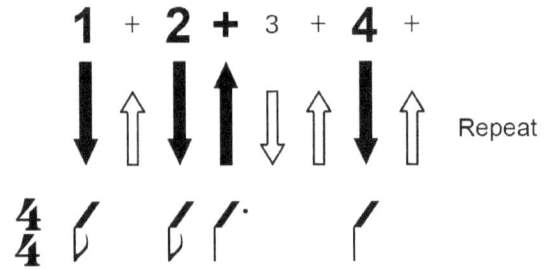

A5.

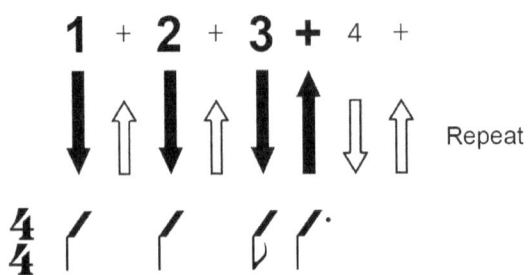

A6.

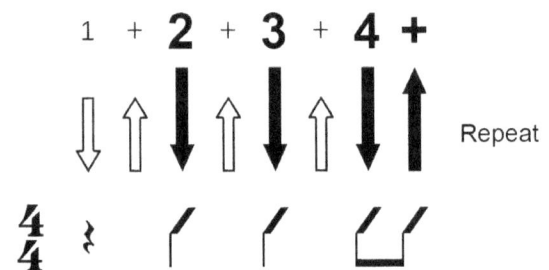

Patterns such as A6 above may have no strum on beat 1, yet it is important to pay attention to beat 1 for awareness of where you are on the repeats. When repeating A6, you can let the strum at the end of the pattern continue to ring over the start of the next repeat until the next

18

strum occurs. In other words on the repeats we ignore the rest symbol. This applies to all patterns, which start with rests (for example A10 and A11).

A7.

A8.

A9.

A10.

Tip: It is important to play these at a speed you can play correctly, which is why it can be a good idea to go slowly at first, particularly as the strumming patterns get more complex.

A11.

A12.

A13.

A14.

Note: When a rhythmic pattern occurs on weaker places (such as on the "ands") in comparison to the stronger numbered beats, this is known as *syncopation*. Many of the above patterns use syncopation, as do the following ones.

With two + in the strumming pattern.

A15.

A16.

A17.

A18.

A19.

A20.

Tip: If you find your strumming hand temporarily stops as you think about what comes next, it can help to exaggerate the movements of the ghost strums to reinforce them in our consciousness and therefore eventually into our coordination. It's similar to how proofreading can be more effective when saying the words you are reading out loud, making it less likely to miss something.

A21.

A22.

With three + in the strumming pattern.

A23.

A24.

A25.

A26.

A27.

A28.

Twenty-eight patterns might not be all the possibilities, but certainly plenty to practise with.

Chord Changes Part I

Shared Fret Locations - 1st and 2nd Fingers

So far we've only used one chord at a time in order to focus solely on strumming. We also need to be able to change between chords while we strum. Now we'll look at some chord changes on their own before using them with various strumming patterns. We will start with some of the easiest chord changes; ones in which there are fretting finger locations shared between chords, meaning that at least one fretting finger can remain in the same place when changing between them.

Strum each chord only once, before changing to, then strumming the next. Keep going back and forth between the pairs of chords like this. Repeating them counts for the reverse of the chord change. In other words repeating C to Am for instance, will give you Am to C when you go back to C from Am for the repeat. There is no specific pace or rhythm required as the point is to practise only changing between chords, therefore if you need to do it slowly at first to get it accurate, all the better. Video articulates this well, so the following chord changes have a video demonstration.

10 ▶

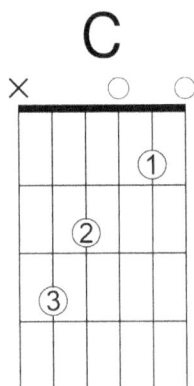

2nd finger remains in same location.

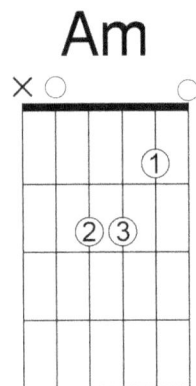

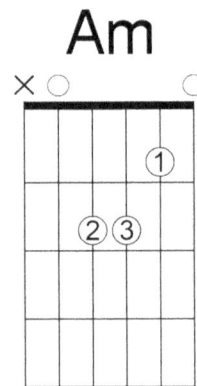

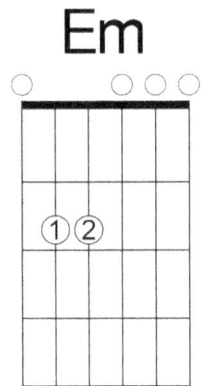

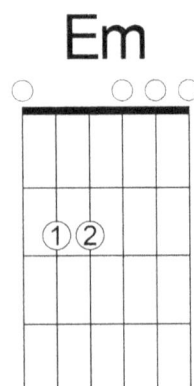

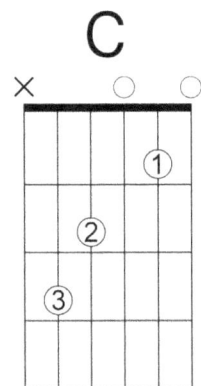

2nd finger remains in same location.

1st finger remains in same location.

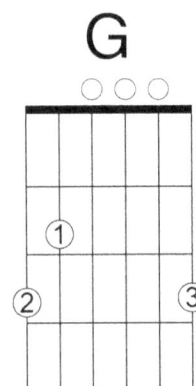

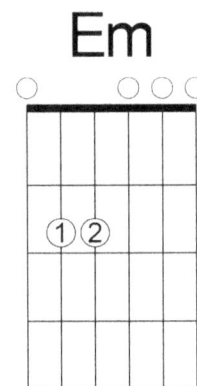

2nd finger remains in same location.

Here are the four sets of chord change pairs on top of each other for you to try one at a time, with the simplest of former strumming patterns (A1). Play at a speed you can manage over the counting audio tracks 1+2+3+4+ or use metronome.

C   **Am**

Am   **Em**

Em   **G**

Em   **C**

1 + 2 + 3 + 4 +   1 + 2 + 3 + 4 +

Repeat

Pre-emptive Chord Changing

If it's a struggle for your fretting hand to move quickly enough to form the next chord in time for when it is to be strummed, then it can help if the fretting hand starts to change chord a bit earlier. A good way to do this is to coordinate the start of changing to the next chord with a prior ghost strum. Referring to the previous exercise we can see that there are ghost strums before every chord change. Below are examples of starting to change chord on either beat 4, or the + after beat 4, both with video demonstrations.

Starting to Change Chord on beat 4

11 ▶

Em   **G**

1 + 2 + 3 + 4 +   1 + 2 + 3 + 4 +

Repeat

Start changing to next Chord here   Start changing to next Chord here

23

Starting to Change Chord on the + after beat 4

12 ▶

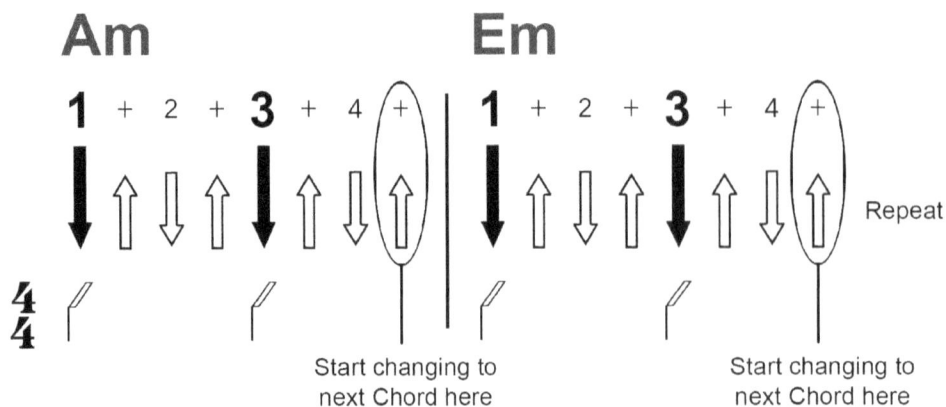

Am   Em

1 + 2 + **3** + 4 (+) | **1** + 2 + **3** + 4 (+)

Repeat

Start changing to
next Chord here

Start changing to
next Chord here

As you will likely have noticed, pre-emptive chord changing results in ending the previous chord slightly early. This is less of an issue if the chords share notes, which segue between the chords when changing. For instance, the chords of C and Am share the same notes on the B and high E strings, or the Em and G chords, which both have open G and B strings. This won't always be the case depending on which chords are used, as there are many chords that don't share notes (as we will see later on in the book). Either way, it will not greatly affect the overall structure and intended sound of the music. That is to say, it is more important to play the next chord where it is supposed to be, than it is for the previous chord to last for its entire duration. That said, if you go *too* far back you risk cutting off too much of the previous chord and not giving it enough time to make its point within the music. This is why I haven't gone as far back as the + before beat 4 in the above examples.

Changing chord on the last ghost strum over the previous chord is a quite standard way of playing (in the case of these exercises that would be the last + after beat 4). For the following, slightly more challenging exercise using strumming pattern A2, a pre-emptive chord change can't begin any earlier than the last + as there is an actual strum on beat 4.

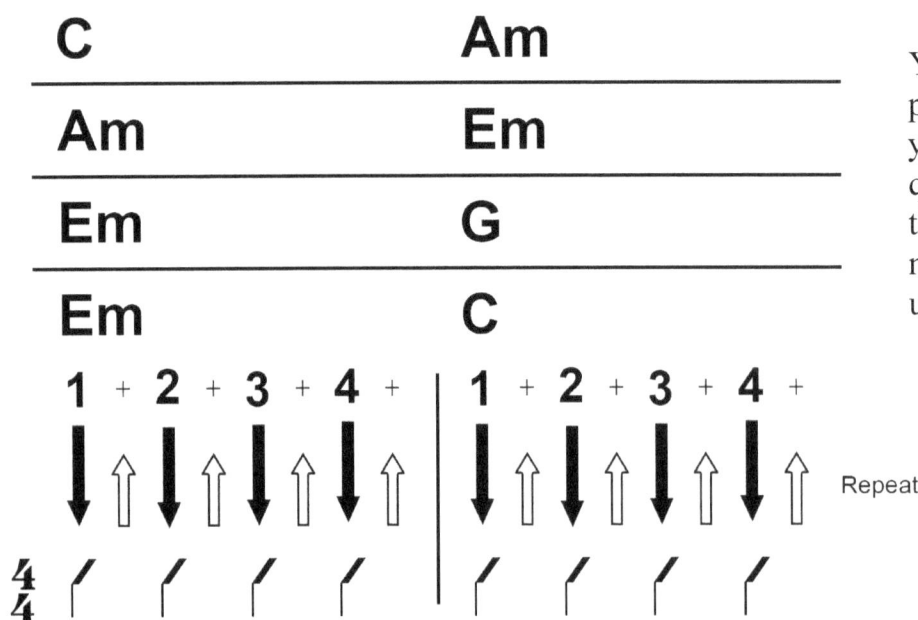

C	Am
Am	Em
Em	G
Em	C

1 + **2** + **3** + **4** + | **1** + **2** + **3** + **4** +

Repeat

You don't *have* to use pre-emptive changes if you can change chords quickly enough keeping the flow of the music. If not, then by all means use it.

Strumming Exercises 1a

1 Chord per Bar

So far we've looked at strumming patterns on their own and some chord changes on their own. Now let's combine strumming patterns with chord changes. As before, repeating the exercises will count for the reverse of the chord change (e.g. repeating C to Am will require Am to C when restarting). Each chord change is shown with two patterns from strumming patterns A as examples.

As these are the first strumming exercises with chord changes there's a video demonstration of the first three at a tempo of 70bpm (70 beats per minute). The audio examples are also at 70bpm but with a simple percussion sound (closed hi-hat) in the background on beats 1, 2, 3 and 4. When trying these yourself, they could be played with the counting audio tracks 1+2+3+4+ at various speeds, or while counting for yourself, or over a metronome.

(Strumming Pattern A5)   (Strumming Pattern A16)

Remember, it can help to coordinate chord changes with a prior ghost strum, as mentioned in Pre-emptive Chord Changing (page 23).

(Strumming Pattern A8)   (Strumming Pattern A22)

(Strumming Pattern A12)   (Strumming Pattern A6)

Note: Regarding the rhythmic notation of the previous two strumming exercises; a tie is used between the last note of the first bar and the first note of the second bar, due to how this note's duration overlaps the bars. Ties are always used for any note that lasts beyond the bar that it starts within.

(Strumming Pattern A17)   (Strumming Pattern A9)

You could also try the above chord changes with any of the other patterns from Strumming Patterns A (page 18). One of the important factors for practise is discovering what you can't do then working on it.

Tip: If you struggle to play a strumming pattern or any part of it, try listening to the example audio but don't play any strums, instead just do ghost strums over it. As you do this, imagine you are actually playing the strums that you hear as your hand moves up and down. This will help bridge the gap making it easier when you attempt the actual strums.

Study Piece 1a

1 Chord per Bar

Time to put everything together into a piece of music. The following study piece (on the next page) has most of the strumming patterns missing for you to decide which to use from Strumming Patterns A (page 18).

Normally, in a real life performance situation you would have to remember the strumming pattern(s) as only the chords would be written down (you might be familiar with this if you have other pieces of music or any songbooks). Thankfully however, a song won't usually have more than a couple of strumming patterns, often only one, therefore you could use the same strumming pattern for all of the missing bars. A little trickier would be two different patterns, such as one strumming pattern for the first half of the piece on lines one and two, then another strumming pattern for the second half on lines three and four. Line five is just a G chord strummed once and sustained, ending the piece.

For the bars where the arrows are kept, keep these simple strumming patterns the same as written. These particular bars allow more time for the following chord changes, while also giving you a short rest. Although your strumming hand won't need to be as animated for the ghost strums of these particular bars, it should still at least bounce down and up a little in order to keep time, therefore making it easier to come in at the right place for the next bar. This will be the same for all forthcoming study pieces where arrows have been kept.

5 🔊))

C **Am** **Em**

1 + 2 + 3 + 4 + | 1 + 2 + 3 + 4 + | 1 + 2 + 3 + 4 + | 1 + 2 + 3 + 4 + ‖ :

4/4

This is a repeat sign. Go back to the beginning and play this line of music again then continue the piece.

G

1 + 2 + 3 + 4 + | 1 + 2 + 3 + 4 + | **1** + 2 + **3** + 4 + | **1** + 2 + 3 + 4 +

Am **Em** **G**

1 + 2 + 3 + 4 + | 1 + 2 + 3 + 4 + | 1 + 2 + 3 + 4 + | 1 + 2 + 3 + 4 +

Em **C** **Am**

1 + 2 + 3 + 4 + | 1 + 2 + 3 + 4 + | 1 + 2 + 3 + 4 + | **1** + 2 + 3 + 4 +

G

1 + 2 + 3 + 4 + | 1 + 2 + 3 + 4 + ‖

The following example, which you may find more challenging, has a different strumming pattern for each line. The first line uses strumming pattern A5, the second line uses pattern A4, the third line uses pattern A8 and the fourth line uses pattern A17.

6

This is a repeat sign. Go back to the beginning and play this line of music again then continue the piece.

You're not expected to come up with your own version with a different strumming pattern for each line (one or two for the previous blank version will suffice), but there's nothing stopping you if you want an even greater challenge.

Chord Changes Part II
Shared Fret Locations - 1st and 2nd Fingers

Here are some new chord changes. They are similar in shape to the ones we've already looked at. In fact, they would be the same if it were not for the part added after each name (e.g. maj7 after C for "Cmaj7" or 7 after Am for "Am7"). These new chords also share similar finger positions, meaning that from one chord to the next, at least one fretting finger can remain in the same place.

14 ▶

Cmaj7   Am7

Am7   Em7

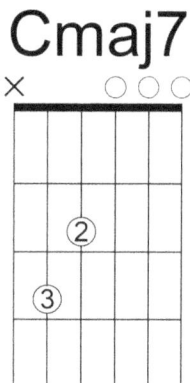

2nd finger remains in same location.

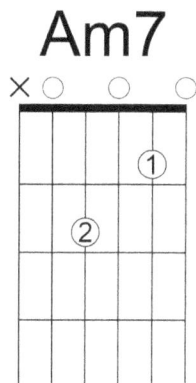

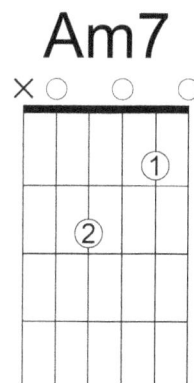

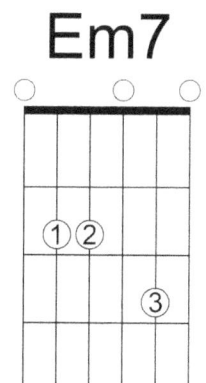

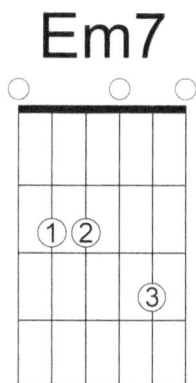

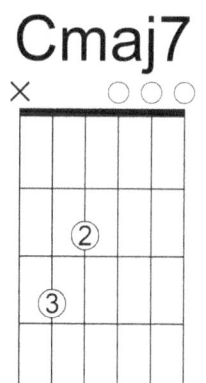

2nd finger remains in same location.

Em7   G6

Em7   Cmaj7

1st finger remains in same location.

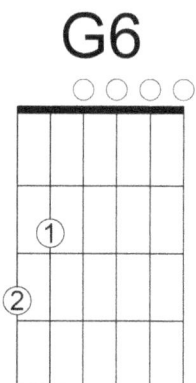

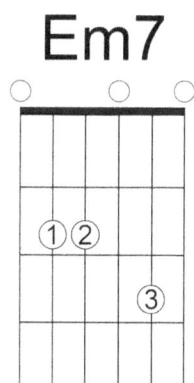

2nd finger remains in same location.

Tip: When you hear a sequence of chords being strummed, it is, of course, the strumming of chords you hear, not the short spaces between the chords in which the fretting hand changes from one to another. Yet without this barely noticeable aspect, it would not be at all possible. The process of changing between chords is much like backstage of a theatre; there are things you don't see or hear that contribute to what you do see and hear, such as the people who work in the Props department. The process of changing from one chord to the next may not be audible but its importance should not be overlooked for a learner. This is why in the video demonstrations I start the chord changes slowly. So, at first, make sure you change between them as slowly as you need in order to make the chords accurate and clear sounding.

Here are those chord changes over the simplest two former strumming patterns A1 then A2. Play over the counting audio tracks 1+2+3+4+ or over a metronome at a speed you can manage.

Cmaj7	Am7
Am7	Em7
Em7	G6
Em7	Cmaj7

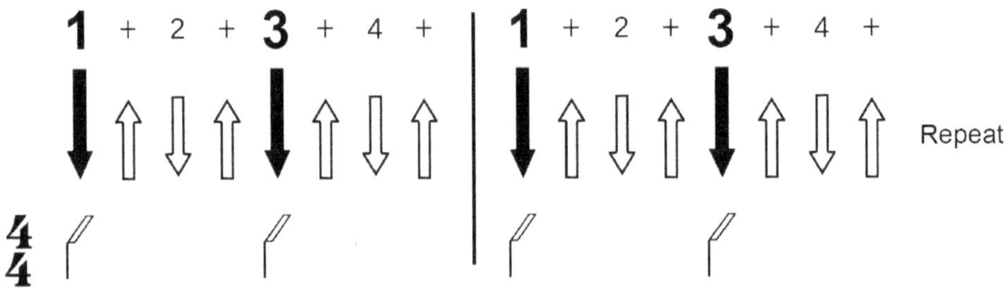

Cmaj7	Am7
Am7	Em7
Em7	G6
Em7	Cmaj7

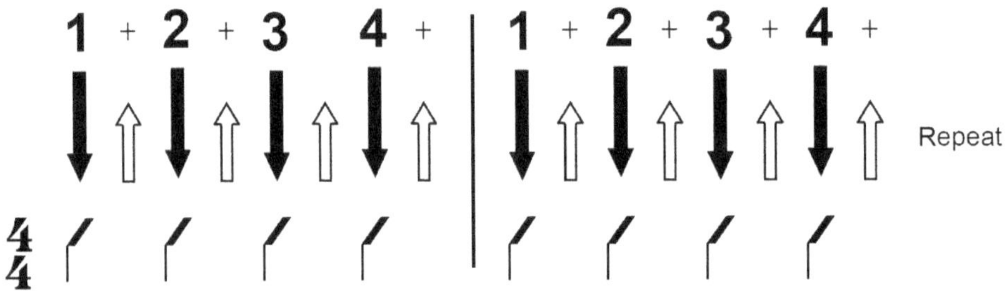

Note: Chord Changes III and upwards will contain too many chords to stack up in a diagram above these strumming patterns, therefore from now on remember that, at first, it can be worth practising chord changes with the simple strumming patterns A1 and A2.

Strumming Exercises 1b

2 Chords per Bar

So far we have dealt with one chord per bar only. Often, songs will share different chords within the same bar. Here are a few strumming exercises in which there are two chords per bar. Each chord change is shown with two patterns from Strumming Patterns A as examples, although you could use any pattern from Strumming Patterns A (page 18). The new chords from Chord Changes Part II are shown directly above the strumming patterns in bold text (the audio examples use these), while the previous chords from Chord Changes Part I are also shown above so you can practise with either chord sequence.

The audio examples are at 70bpm (in fact all of the strumming exercise audio examples in this book are at 70bpm). When trying these yourself, the exercises could be played with the counting audio tracks 1+2+3+4+ at various speeds, or while counting for yourself, or over a metronome.

(Strumming Pattern A3)

(Strumming Pattern A8)

(Strumming Pattern A15)

(Strumming Pattern A17)

Note: The second chord is always above beat 3 as this is where the chord is considered to start. At what point the second chord is actually strummed depends on the particular strumming pattern used. For example, in the two previous exercises the Em7 chord is written above beat three, but isn't played until the + after beat 3 in the first of the above two exercises, while in the second of the above two exercises it isn't strummed until beat 4. The same will apply to the forthcoming study pieces when there are two chords in any bar.

Em   G

Em7   **G6**

1 + 2 **+** 3 **+ 4** +

4/4

(Strumming Pattern A16)

Em   G

Em7   **G6**

1 + **2** + **3 + 4** +

4/4

(Strumming Pattern A7)

Em   C

Em7   **Cmaj7**

1 + 2 **+** 3 **+ 4** +

4/4

(Strumming Pattern A23)

Em   C

Em7   **Cmaj7**

1 **+ 2** + **3 + 4** +

4/4

(Strumming Pattern A20)

Study Piece 1b

1 & 2 Chords per Bar

In practise, the amount of chords in a bar is determined by what sounds best as the composer intends. For this reason, even though the previous strumming exercises all have two chords per bar, for the following study piece only some of its bars have two chords.

The new chords are shown in the usual place above the bars, while the original chords from Chord Changes Part I are also included in brackets above the new chords so you could use those if you wish before moving onto the new chords. Occasionally both sets of chords happen to be the same (such as Em at the end of the first line). Both sets of chords will work over the same backing track.

As before, you could use a pattern of your choice from Strumming Patterns A (page 18) for all of the missing bars. A little trickier would be two different patterns, such as one strumming pattern for lines one and two, then another strumming pattern for lines three and four. Keep the strumming as written where the arrows have been kept.

(C) **Cmaj7** (Am) **Am7** (Em) **Em7** (G) **G6** (Em) **Em**

1 + 2 + 3 + 4 + | 1 + 2 + 3 + 4 + | 1 + 2 + 3 + 4 + | 1 + 2 + 3 + 4 +

$\frac{4}{4}$

(G) **G**

1 + 2 + 3 + 4 + | 1 + 2 + 3 + 4 + | **1** + 2 + **3** + 4 + | **1** + 2 + 3 + 4 +

(Am) **Am7** (Em) **Em7** (G) **G6** (Em) **Em**

1 + 2 + 3 + 4 + | 1 + 2 + 3 + 4 + | 1 + 2 + 3 + 4 + | 1 + 2 + 3 + 4 +

(Em) **Em7** (C) **Cmaj7** (Am) **Am7**

1 + 2 + 3 + 4 + | 1 + 2 + 3 + 4 + | 1 + 2 + 3 + 4 + | **1** + 2 + 3 + 4 +

(G) **G**

1 + 2 + 3 + 4 + | 1 + 2 + 3 + 4 +

The next example, which you may find more challenging, has a different strumming pattern for each line of the piece. The first line uses strumming pattern A15, the second line uses pattern A16, the third line uses pattern A8 and the fourth line uses pattern A17.

It's not necessary for you to come up with your own version that uses a different strumming pattern for each line, although there's nothing stopping you if you want an even greater challenge. One or two patterns, as mentioned for the previous blank version will suffice.

Chord Changes Part III

Shared Fret Locations - 3rd Finger

Here are some new chord changes. Like the last ones they share similar finger positions so that from one chord to the next at least one fretting finger can remain in the same place.

15 ▶

Dm   **Cadd9**

Cadd9   **G**

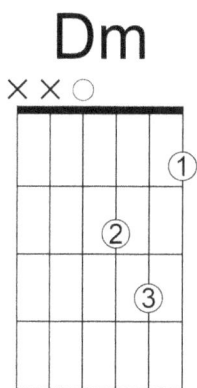

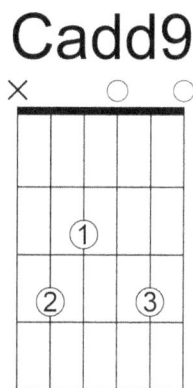

3rd finger remains in same location.

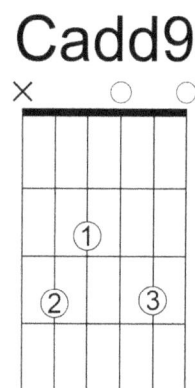

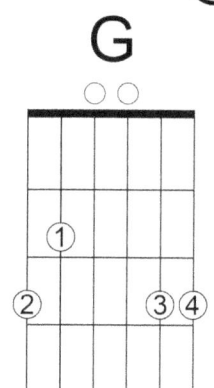

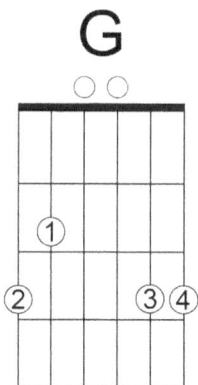

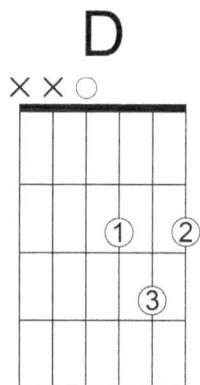

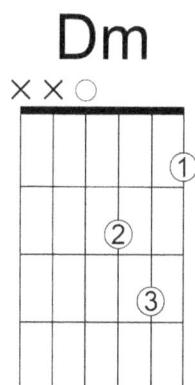

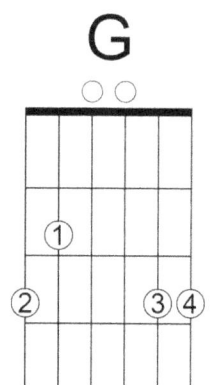

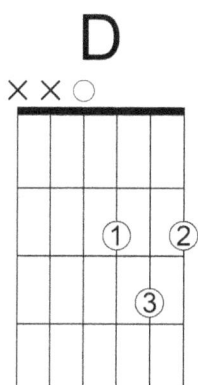

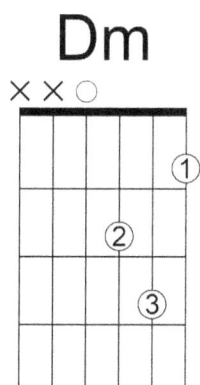

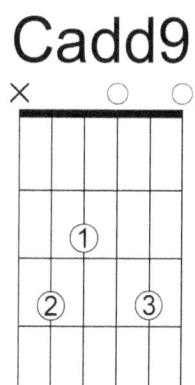

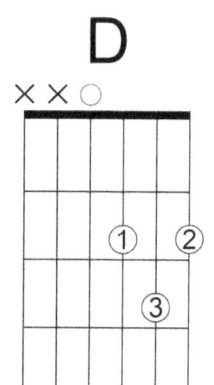

3rd finger remains in same location.

G   **D**

Dm   **G**

3rd finger remains in same location.

3rd finger remains in same location.

D   **Dm**

Cadd9   **D**

3rd finger remains in same location.

3rd finger remains in same location.

Strumming Patterns B

A Strum on the + after Beat 4

So far all the chord changes we have dealt with have been a quarter note apart, meaning there has always been at least one ghost strum before the chord change. Changing chords between eighth notes however, allows half as much time. By repeating the following patterns, the strum on the + after beat 4 and the strum on beat 1 of the next repeat are next to each other, an eighth note apart. This is where you would change chord from one bar to the next. There are no chord changes yet but try these strumming patterns with a chord of your choice. Any of the former chords would do. Like Strumming Patterns A, these can also be played with counting audio tracks 1+2+3+4+ at various speeds, or while counting for yourself, or you could use a metronome, whichever you prefer. The first three start off with one + in the strumming pattern.

B1.

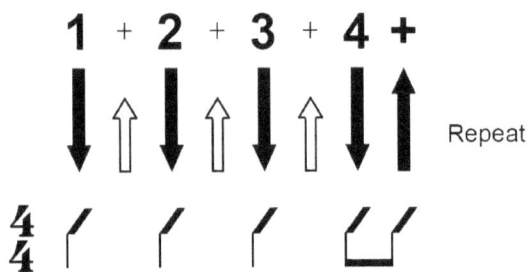

B2.

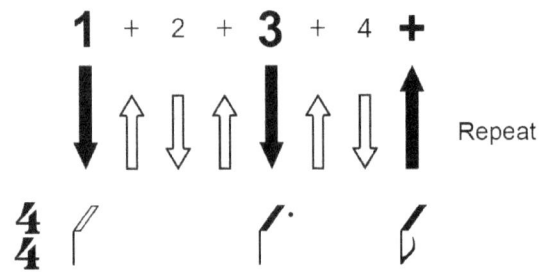

With two + in the strumming pattern.

B3.

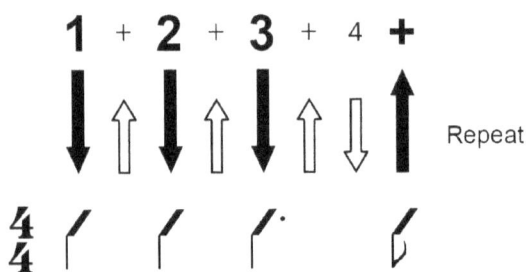

B4.

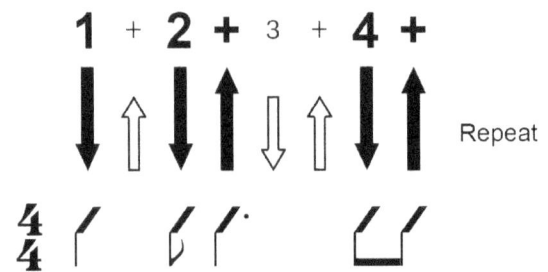

B5.

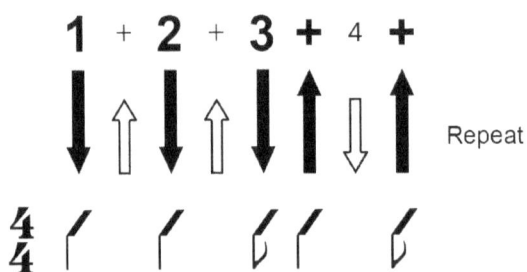

B6.

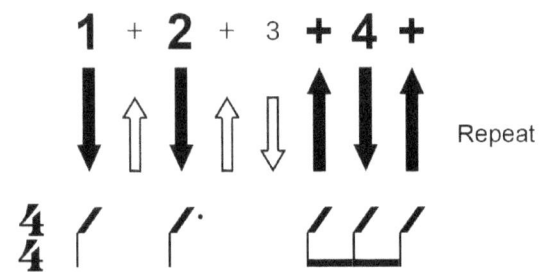

B7.

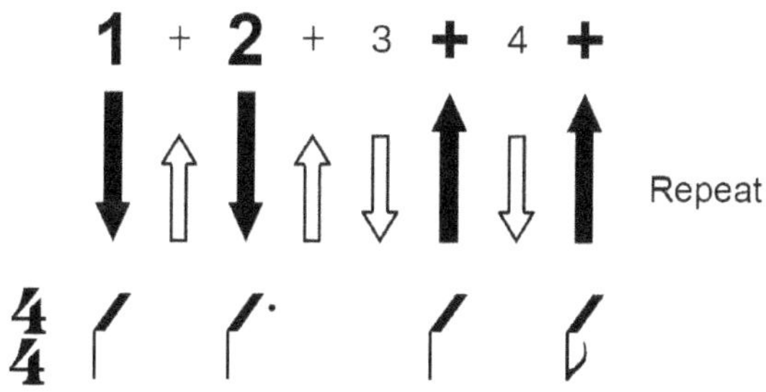

1 + 2 + 3 + 4 +

Repeat

$\frac{4}{4}$

B8.

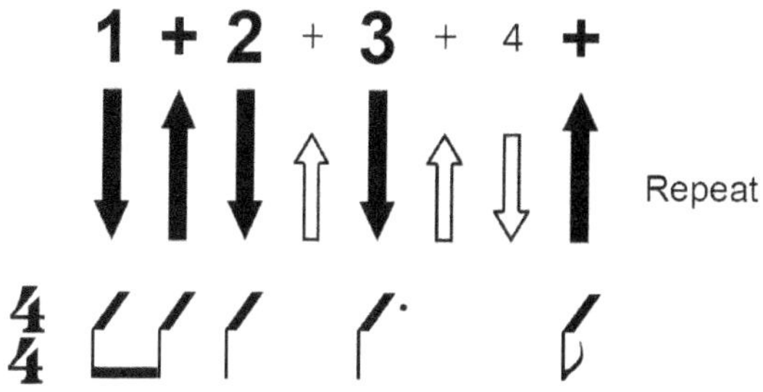

1 + 2 + 3 + 4 +

Repeat

$\frac{4}{4}$

B9.

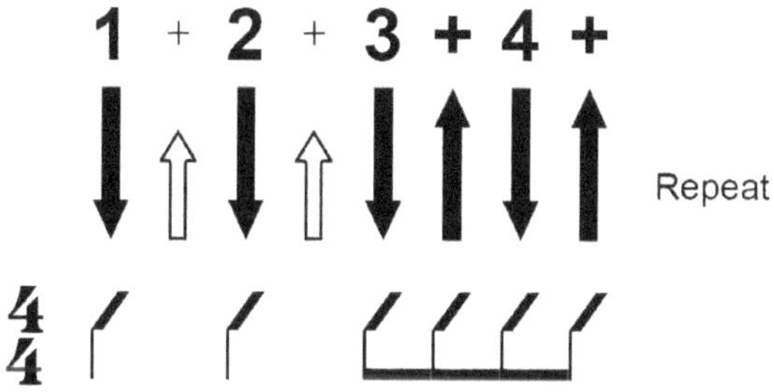

1 + 2 + 3 + 4 +

Repeat

$\frac{4}{4}$

B10.

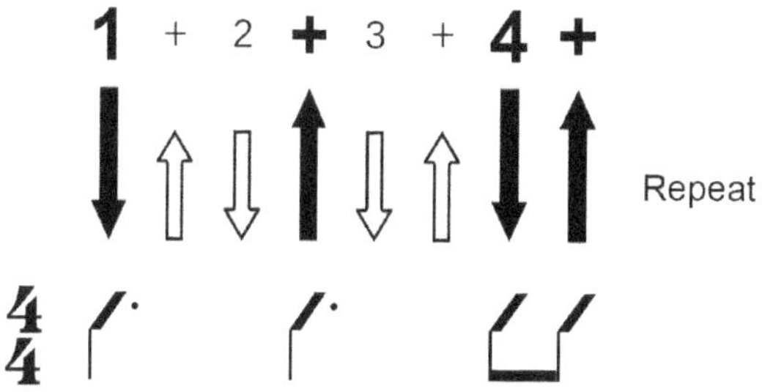

1 + 2 + 3 + 4 +

Repeat

$\frac{4}{4}$

B11.

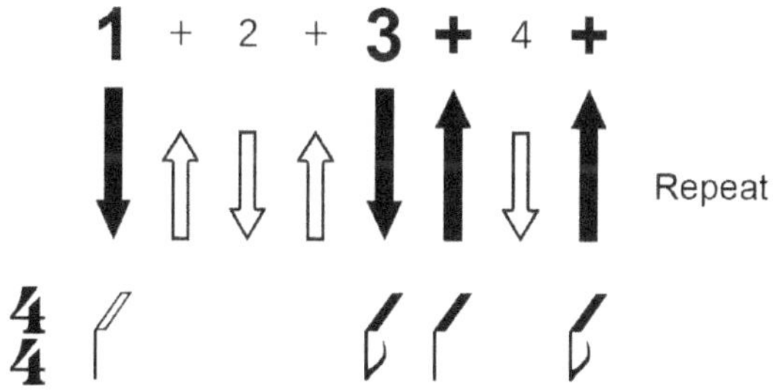

1 + 2 + 3 + 4 +

Repeat

$\frac{4}{4}$

B12.

1 + 2 + 3 + 4 +

Repeat

$\frac{4}{4}$

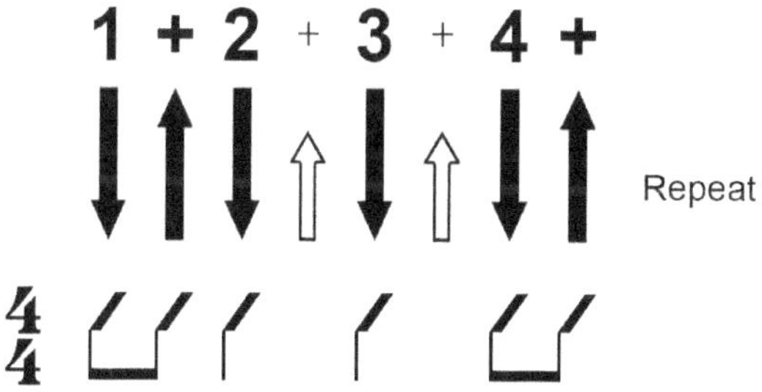

With three + in the strumming pattern.

B13.

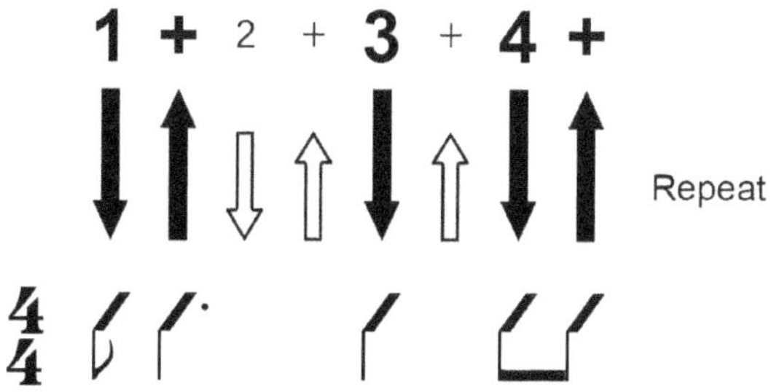

1 + 2 + 3 + 4 +

Repeat

$\frac{4}{4}$

B14.

1 + 2 + 3 + 4 +

Repeat

$\frac{4}{4}$

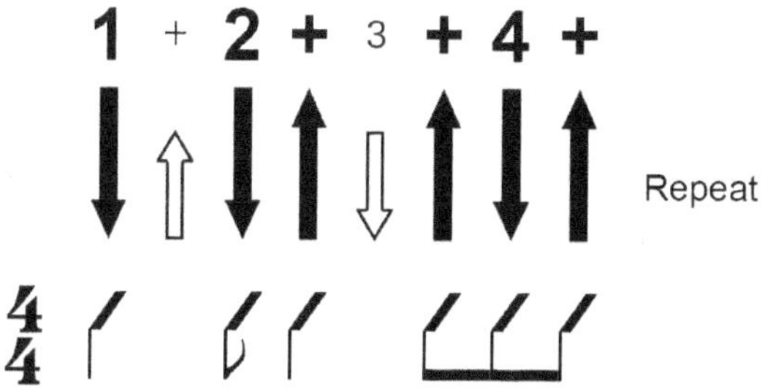

B15.

B16.

B17.

B18.

With four + in the strumming pattern.

B19.

B20.

B21.

B22.

Strumming Exercises 2a

1 Chord per Bar

Now for a few strumming exercises with chord changes occurring between eighth notes from one bar to the next. It won't be possible to change chord as early as was explained in the previous section titled Pre-emptive Chord Changing (page 23). The new chords from Chord Changes Part III are shown directly above the strumming patterns, while the previous chords are also shown above those so you have a variety of options to practise. When trying these for yourself, the exercises could be played with the counting audio tracks 1+2+3+4+ at various speeds, or while counting for yourself, or over a metronome.

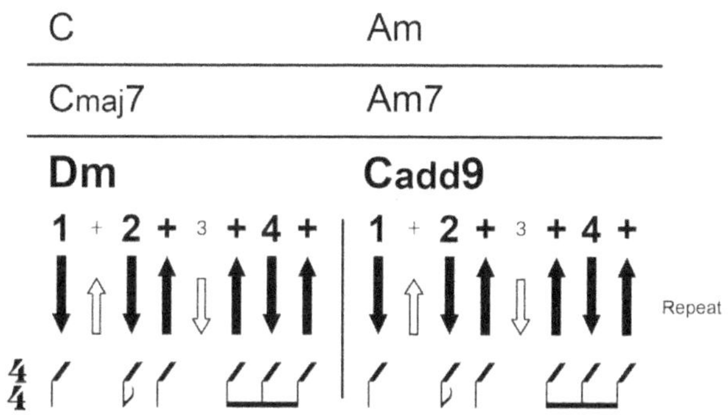

(Strumming Pattern B14)

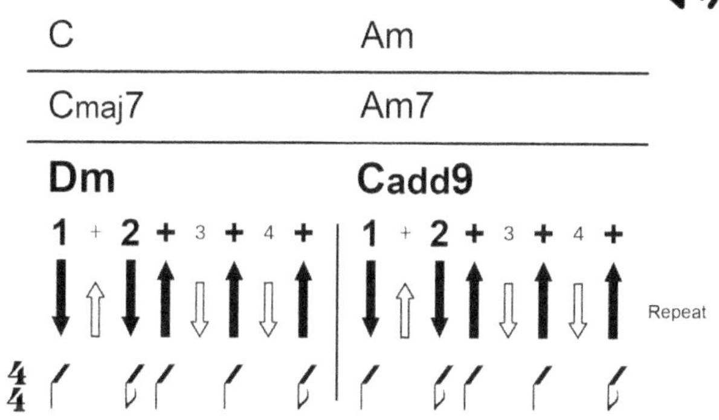

(Strumming Pattern B19)

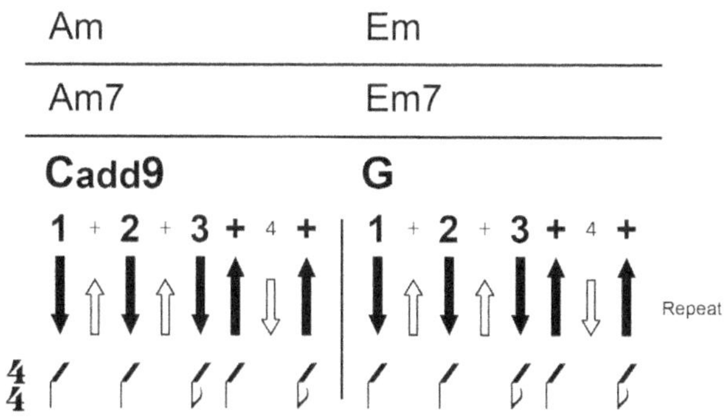

(Strumming Pattern B5)

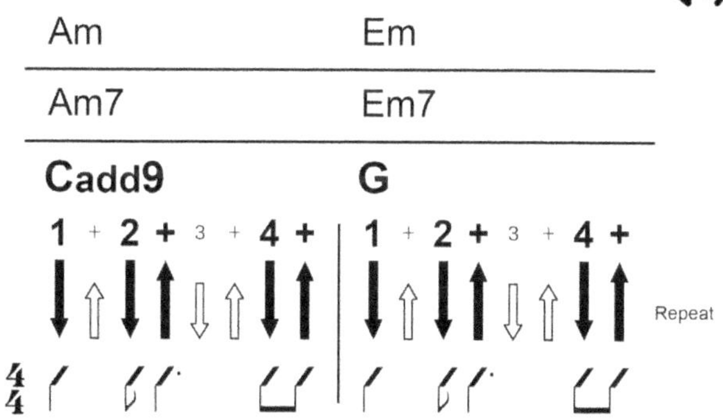

(Strumming Pattern B4)

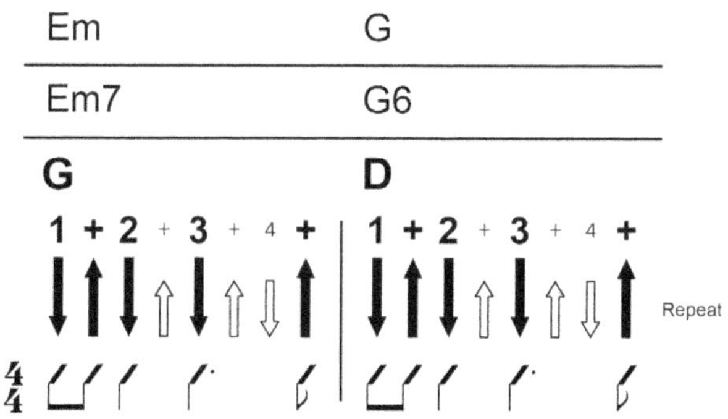

(Strumming Pattern B8)

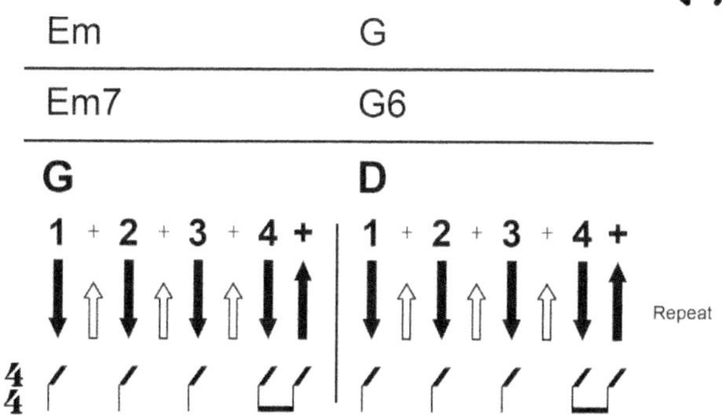

(Strumming Pattern B1)

Am	C
Am7	Cmaj7
D	Dm

1 + 2 + 3 + 4 + | 1 + 2 + 3 + 4 +

4/4 (Repeat)

(Strumming Pattern B7)

Am	C
Am7	Cmaj7
D	Dm

1 + 2 + 3 + 4 + | 1 + 2 + 3 + 4 +

4/4 (Repeat)

(Strumming Pattern B3)

Em	C
Em7	Cmaj7
Dm	G

1 + 2 + 3 + 4 + | 1 + 2 + 3 + 4 +

4/4 (Repeat)

(Strumming Pattern B2)

Em	C
Em7	Cmaj7
Dm	G

1 + 2 + 3 + 4 + | 1 + 2 + 3 + 4 +

4/4 (Repeat)

(Strumming Pattern B9)

Some examples of songs, which contain chords that share the same finger locations, would be "Wonderwall" or "Roll With It" by the band Oasis or the starting chords of the song "Zombie" by the band The Cranberries.

Study Piece 2a

1 Chord per Bar

For the following study piece the new chords (from Chord Changes Part III) are shown in the usual place above the bars. The previous chords (from Chord Changes Part II) are also included in brackets above the new chords. Both sets of chords will *not* work over the same backing track so a separate backing track has been made for "Study Piece 2a Chord Changes II".

You could use the same strumming pattern from Strumming Patterns B (Page 36) for all of the missing bars. A little trickier would be two different patterns from Strumming Patterns B, such as one pattern for lines one and two, then another pattern for lines three and four. You could even use a pattern from Strumming Patterns A (page 18) if you feel like you still need more practise with changing chords between quarter notes while using the new chords, although this won't have any chord changes between eighth notes.

(Cmaj7)
Dm

(Am7)
Cadd9

(Em7)
G

1 + 2 + 3 + 4 + | 1 + 2 + 3 + 4 + | 1 + 2 + 3 + 4 + | 1 + 2 + 3 + 4 +

$\frac{4}{4}$

(G6)
D

1 + 2 + 3 + 4 + | 1 + 2 + 3 + 4 + | **1** + 2 + **3** + 4 + | **1** + 2 + 3 + 4 +

(Am7)
Cadd9

(Em7)
G

(G6)
D

1 + 2 + 3 + 4 + | 1 + 2 + 3 + 4 + | 1 + 2 + 3 + 4 + | 1 + 2 + 3 + 4 +

(Em7)
Dm

(Cmaj7)
G

(Am7)
Cadd9

1 + 2 + 3 + 4 + | 1 + 2 + 3 + 4 + | 1 + 2 + 3 + 4 + | **1** + 2 + 3 + 4 +

(G6)
D

1 + 2 + 3 + 4 + | 1 + 2 + 3 + 4 +

The next example, which you may find more challenging, has a different strumming pattern for each line of the piece. The first line uses strumming pattern B14, the second line uses pattern B5, the third line uses pattern B8 and the fourth line uses pattern B2.

(Cmaj7)
Dm

(Am7)
Cadd9

(Em7)
G

(G6)
D

(Am7)
Cadd9

(Em7)
G

(G6)
D

(Em7)
Dm

(Cmaj7)
G

(Am7)
Cadd9

(G6)
D

You are not expected to come up with your own version that uses a different strumming pattern for each line (one or two patterns for the previous blank version will suffice), but there's nothing stopping you if you want an even greater challenge.

Strumming Patterns C

A Strum on the + before Beat 3

Now we'll look at changing between chords on eighth notes when there are two chords in the same bar. All of the following strumming patterns have a strum on the + before beat 3 and a strum on beat 3 itself. This will be the point at which the chord will change halfway through the bar, an eighth note apart. There are no chord changes yet but try these strumming patterns with a chord of your choice. Any of the former chords will do.

As before, these patterns can be played with counting audio tracks 1+2+3+4+ at various speeds, or while counting for yourself, or you could use a metronome, whichever you prefer. The first two start off with one + in the strumming pattern.

C1.

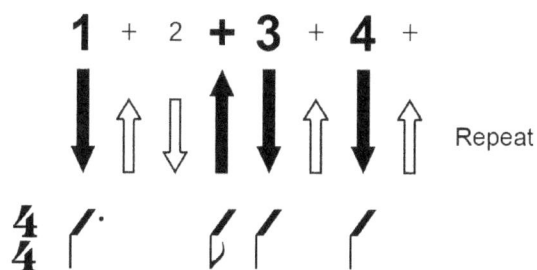

C2.

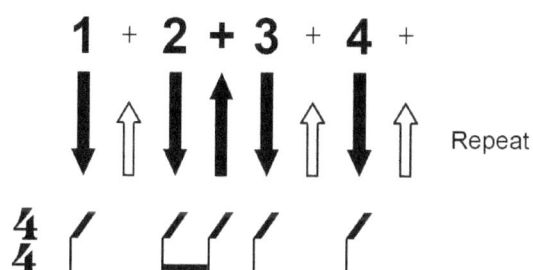

Now with two + in the strumming pattern.

C3.

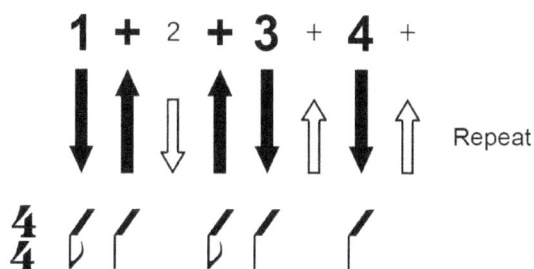

C4.

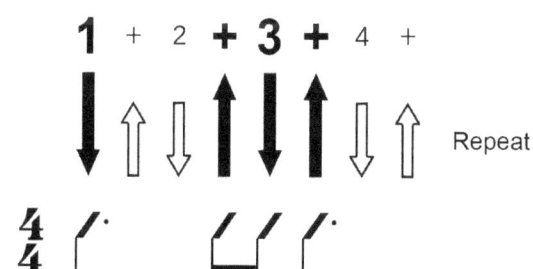

C5.

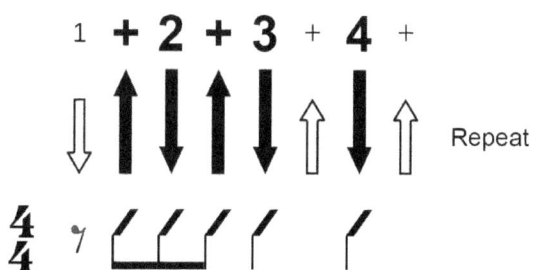

C6.

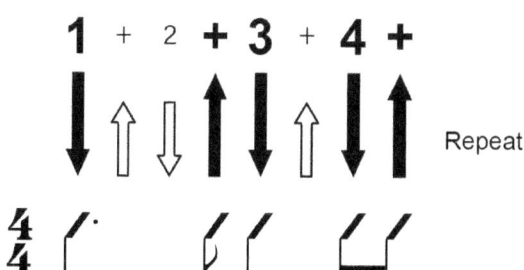

C7.

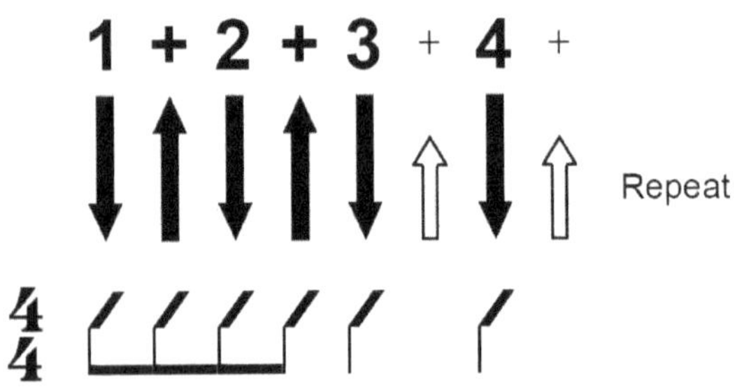

1 + 2 + 3 + 4 +

$\frac{4}{4}$

C8.

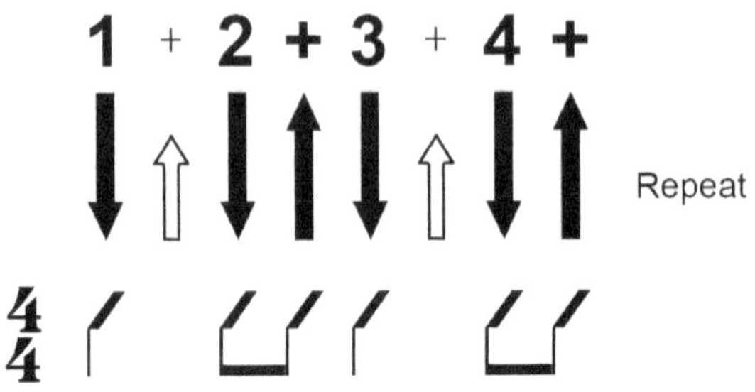

1 + **2 + 3** + **4 +**

Repeat

$\frac{4}{4}$

C9.

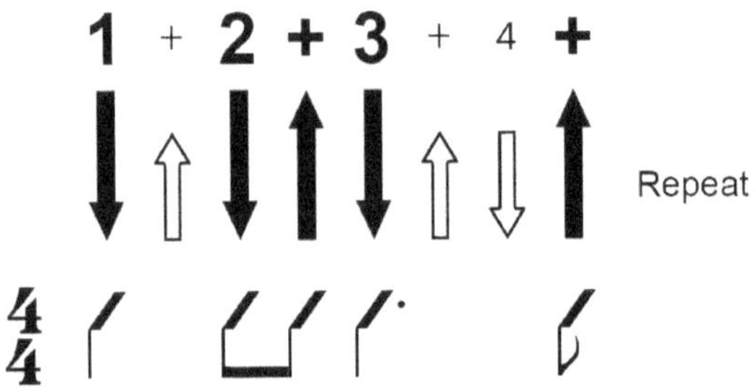

1 + **2 + 3** + 4 **+**

Repeat

$\frac{4}{4}$

C10.

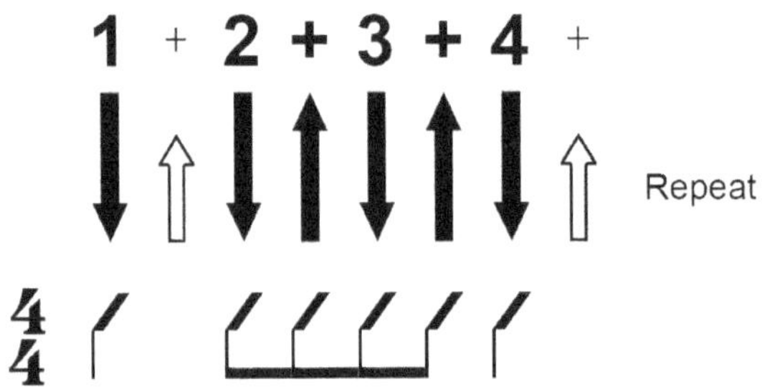

1 + **2 + 3 + 4** +

Repeat

$\frac{4}{4}$

C11.

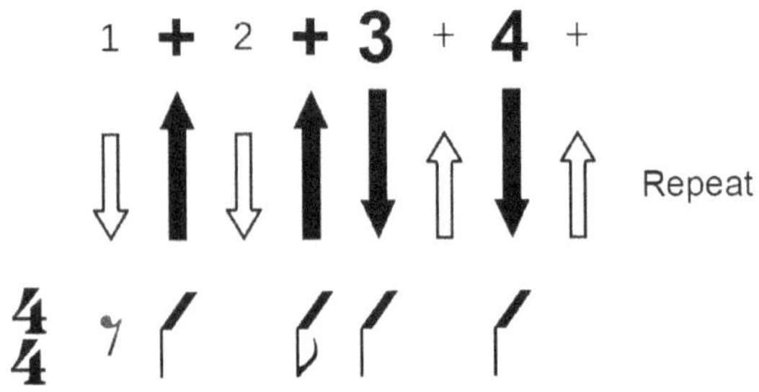

1 **+** 2 **+ 3** + **4** +

Repeat

$\frac{4}{4}$

C12.

1 + 2 **+ 3 + 4** +

Repeat

$\frac{4}{4}$

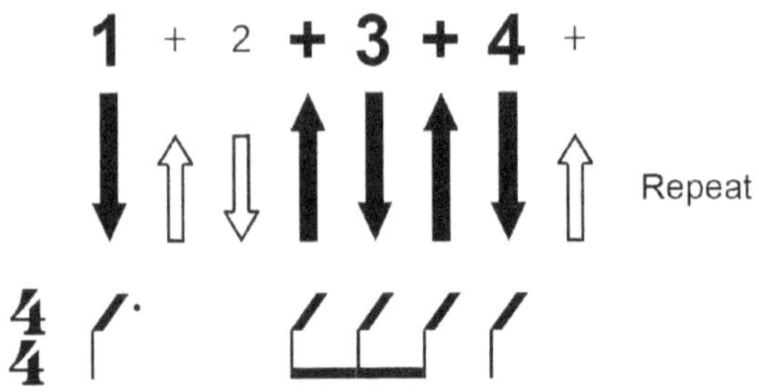

With three + in the strumming pattern.

C13.

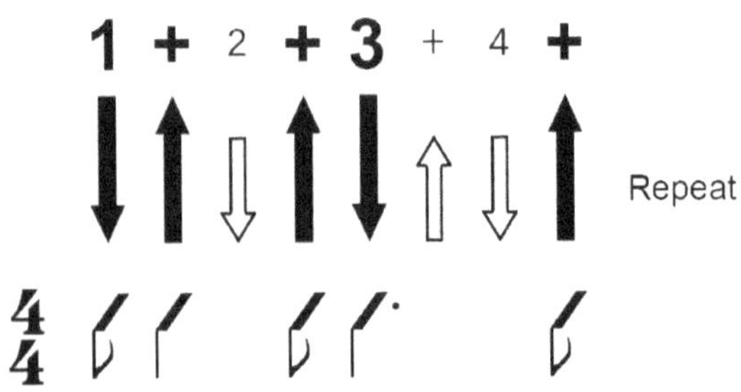

1 + 2 **+ 3** + 4 **+**

Repeat

$\frac{4}{4}$

C14.

1 + 2 **+ 3 +** 4 +

Repeat

$\frac{4}{4}$

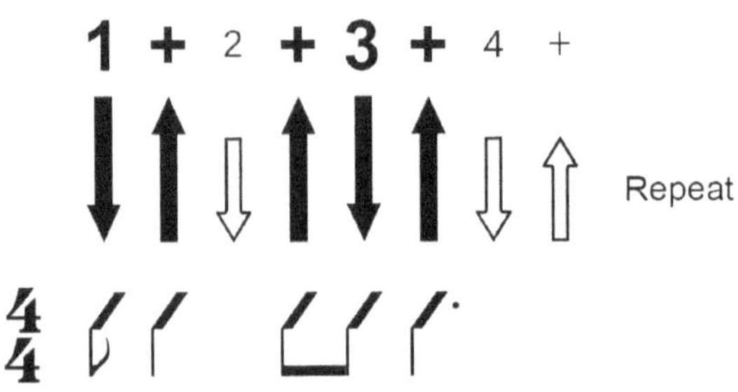

C15.

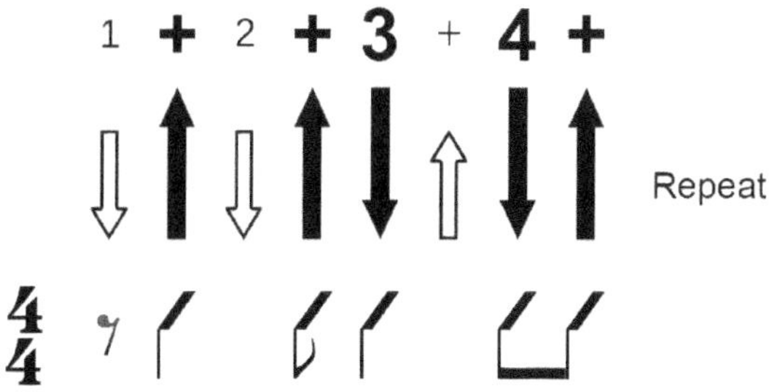

1 **+** 2 **+ 3** + **4 +**

↓ ↑ ↓ ↑ ↓ ↑ ↓ ↓   Repeat

C16.

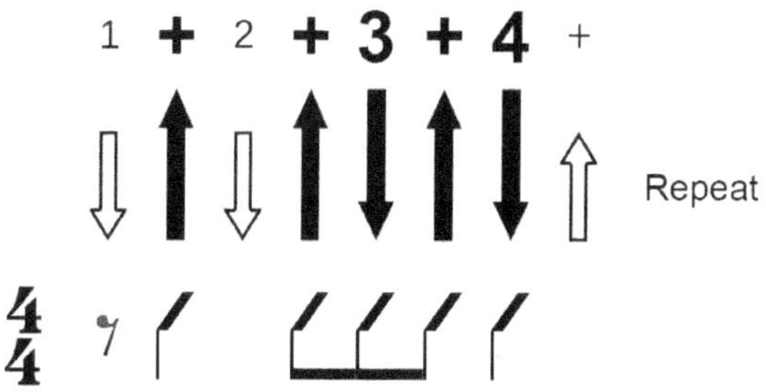

1 **+** 2 **+ 3** + **4** +

↓ ↑ ↓ ↑ ↓ ↓ ↓ ↑   Repeat

C17.

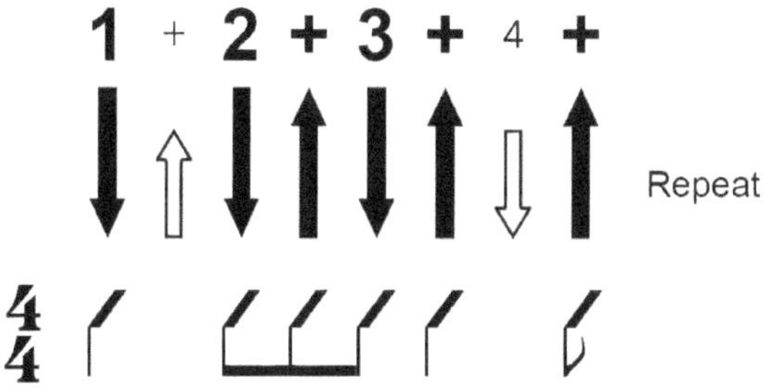

1 + **2 + 3** + 4 **+**

↓ ↑ ↓ ↑ ↓ ↑ ↓ ↑   Repeat

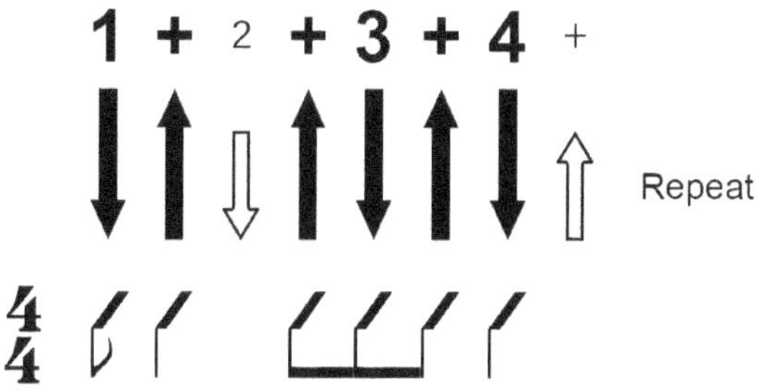

With four **+** in the strumming pattern.

C18.

1 + 2 **+ 3** + **4** +

↓ ↑ ↓ ↑ ↓ ↑ ↓ ↑   Repeat

C19.

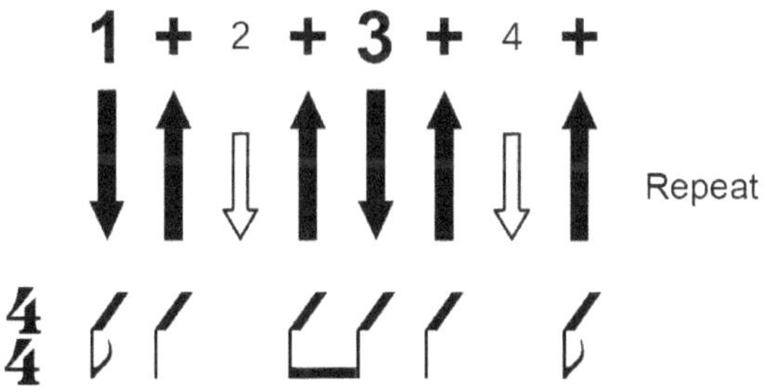

1 + 2 **+ 3** + 4 **+**

↓ ↑ ↓ ↑ ↓ ↑ ↓ ↑   Repeat

C20.

1 + **2** + **3** + 4 **+**

↓ ↑ ↓ ↑ ↓ ↑ ↓ ↑   Repeat

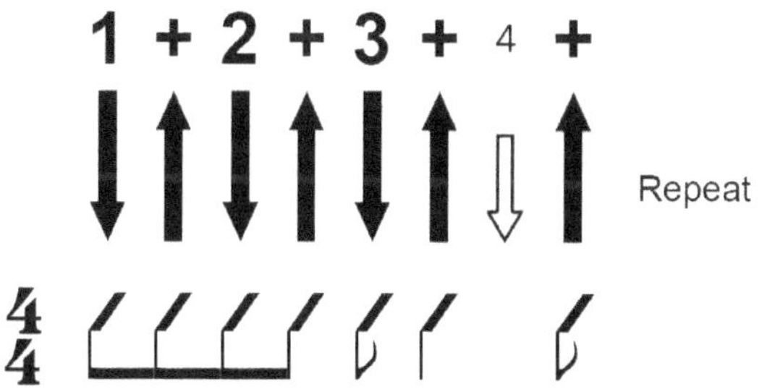

Strumming Exercises 2b

2 Chords per Bar

Here are a few strumming exercises in which there are two chords per bar and the change from one to the other is between eighth notes. When repeated, some of the exercises will also include the equivalent of chord changes between eighth notes from one bar to the next, due to there sometimes being a strum on the "+" after beat 4. The current chords from Chord Changes Part III are used, while previous ones are also shown above so you have a variety of options to practise.

As before, when trying these yourself, the exercises could be played with the counting audio tracks 1+2+3+4+ at various speeds, or while counting for yourself, or over a metronome.

1 🔊

C	Am
Cmaj7	Am7
Dm	**Cadd9**

(Strumming Pattern C9)

C	Am
Cmaj7	Am7
Dm	**Cadd9**

(Strumming Pattern C5)

2 🔊

Am	Em
Am7	Em7
Cadd9 G	

(Strumming Pattern C15)

Am	Em
Am7	Em7
Cadd9 G	

(Strumming Pattern C3)

3 🔊

Em	G
Em7	G6
G	**D**

(Strumming Pattern C2)

Em	G
Em7	G6
G	**D**

(Strumming Pattern C16)

Em	C
Em7	Cmaj7

Dm   G

1 + 2 + 3 + 4 +

4/4

(Strumming Pattern C1)

Em	C
Em7	Cmaj7

Dm   G

1 + 2 + 3 + 4 +

4/4

(Strumming Pattern C19)

G	Em
G6	Em7

Cadd9 D

1 + 2 + 3 + 4 +

4/4

(Strumming Pattern C13)

G	Em
G6	Em7

Cadd9 D

1 + 2 + 3 + 4 +

4/4

(Strumming Pattern C17)

Study Piece 2b

1 & 2 Chords per Bar

For the following study piece, the chords from Chord Changes Part III are shown in the usual place above the bars. The previous chords (from Chord Changes Part II) are also included in brackets above the new chords so you could stick to those for the time being if you prefer while getting used to mid bar chord changes between eighth notes. Both sets of chords will *not* work over the same backing track so a separate backing track has been made for "Study Piece 2b Chord Changes II".

You could use the same strumming pattern from Strumming Patterns C (page 43) for all of the missing bars. A little trickier would be two different patterns, such as one strumming pattern for lines one and two, then another strumming pattern for lines three and four.

(Cmaj7)
Dm

(Am7) (Em7)
Cadd9

(G6)
G

(Em)
Cadd9

1 + 2 + 3 + 4 + | 1 + 2 + 3 + 4 + | 1 + 2 + 3 + 4 + | 1 + 2 + 3 + 4 +

$\frac{4}{4}$

(G)
D

1 + 2 + 3 + 4 + | 1 + 2 + 3 + 4 + | **1** + 2 + **3** + 4 + | **1** + 2 + 3 + 4 +

(Am7)
Cadd9

(Em7)
G

(G6)
D

(Em)
G

1 + 2 + 3 + 4 + | 1 + 2 + 3 + 4 + | 1 + 2 + 3 + 4 + | 1 + 2 + 3 + 4 +

(Em7) (Cmaj7)
Dm G

(Am7)
Cadd9

(Am7)
G

1 + 2 + 3 + 4 + | 1 + 2 + 3 + 4 + | 1 + 2 + 3 + 4 + | **1** + 2 + 3 + 4 +

(G)
D

1 + 2 + 3 + 4 + | 1 + 2 + 3 + 4 +

You could even use a pattern from Strumming Patterns A (page 18) or Strumming Patterns B (page 36), although these won't result in any mid bar chord changes that are between eighth notes.

The following example, which you may find more challenging, has a different strumming pattern for each line of the piece. The first line uses strumming pattern C9, the second line uses pattern C15, the third line uses pattern C2 and the fourth line uses pattern C1.

You are not expected to come up with your own version that uses a different strumming pattern for each line (one or two patterns for the previous blank version will suffice), but there's nothing stopping you if you want an even greater challenge.

You may, by now, have noticed stamina issues in your hands. The irony of practising at slower speeds for beginners is that you'll be holding down chords for longer. Don't overdo it and do take small breaks, particularly if you are using a steel string acoustic.

Summary

All of the things covered so far will be used throughout the rest of the book without need for further explanation. Here's a summary of what we should now be accustomed to.

- The basics of strumming technique and rhythm. When strumming, the hand should move consistently with the beat by using both ghost strums and actual strums.

- Rhythmic note values: whole notes, half notes, quarter notes, eighth notes, dotted notes and equivalent rests.

- When changing between chords that have similar finger positions, it is best to keep those finger positions the same between the chords (Chord Changes Parts I, II and III).

- Pre-emptive chord changing.

- Strumming chord changes between quarter notes from one bar to the next (1a)

- Strumming chord changes between quarter notes when two chords are within the same bar (1b)

- Strumming chord changes between eighth notes from one bar to the next (2a)

- Strumming chord changes between eighth notes when two chords are within the same bar (2b)

Chord Changes Part IV

Relocating with Same Shape

As previously explained, when changing between chords, it is best to maintain the same finger positions wherever possible. However, it is not always the case that chords share finger positions. There are many more chords than the ones used in the previous chapters. The following chord changes require relocation of all their fretting fingers, although they do share the same shape, meaning the fretting fingers can move together in the same formation from one chord to the next.

Make sure you have control of the pressure required in the fretting fingers, ensuring enough when fretting a chord and enough release of pressure when moving to the next. The video example demonstrates this with the first two of the following chord changes (E to Fmaj7#11/E and Am to Fmaj7#11/E).

16 ▶

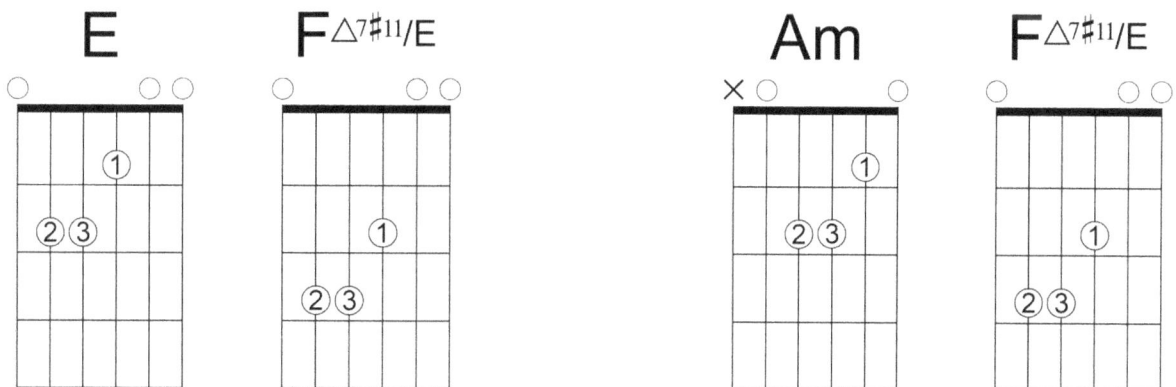

Note: The triangle in the above chord title is an abbreviation for major 7th. The full name for this particular chord is F major 7 sharp 11 over E. The slash line followed by the letter "E" in that chord (as well for as the G6/E chord below) means the lowest bass note of the chord is E, which is why both of these chords keep the same open low E string.

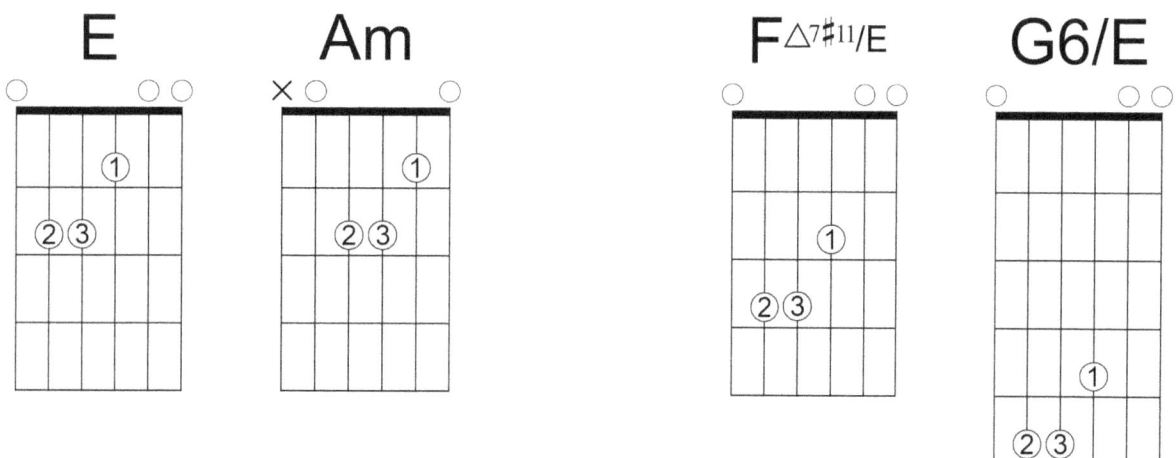

G6/E   E

At first, it can be worth practising the chord change pairs with the simple strumming patterns A1 and A2 over counting audio tracks 1+2+3+4+ or a metronome. Strumming pattern A1 is simply strumming on beats 1 and 3 while A2 is strumming on beats 1, 2, 3 and 4.

Strumming Exercises 3a

1 Chord per Bar

Here are some strumming exercises using the new chords from Chord Changes Part IV. Notice that each chord's bar uses a different strumming pattern, so that not only are we moving from one chord to the next, but also moving between different strumming patterns.

When trying these yourself, the exercises could be played with the counting audio tracks 1+2+3+4+ at various speeds, or while counting for yourself, or over a metronome. This applies to all forthcoming strumming exercises in this book (3b, 4a, 4b, 5a and 5b).

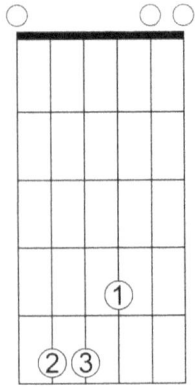

(Strumming Pattern A18 & C11)

(Strumming Pattern A17 & C12)

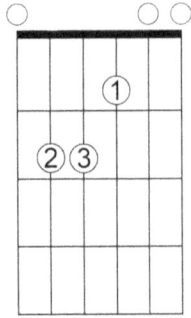

(Strumming Pattern A24 & A19)

(Strumming Pattern B14 & A14)

E   **Am**

(Strumming Pattern A19 & A23)

E   **Am**

(Strumming Pattern A15 & A9)

F△7#11/E   **G6/E**

(Strumming Pattern A23 & C12)

F△7#11/E   **G6/E**

(Strumming Pattern A10 & A26)

G6/E   **E**

(Strumming Pattern C12 & A23)

G6/E   **E**

(Strumming Pattern C3 & C16)

Tip: If you struggle, don't forget the method of only moving the hand as ghost strums over the track at first and imagine you are playing on those parts. This was originally explained on page 26.

Study Piece 3a

1 Chord per Bar

For the following Spanish style study piece the new chords (from Chord Changes Part IV) are used. You can choose your own pair of strumming patterns to go back and forth between them for the entire piece. If you would like a demonstration of moving between two strumming patterns in a piece of music, you could read / listen to the example piece after this one, which has its patterns filled in. The pattern(s) you could use can be from Strumming Patterns A (page 18), B (page 36) or C (page 43).

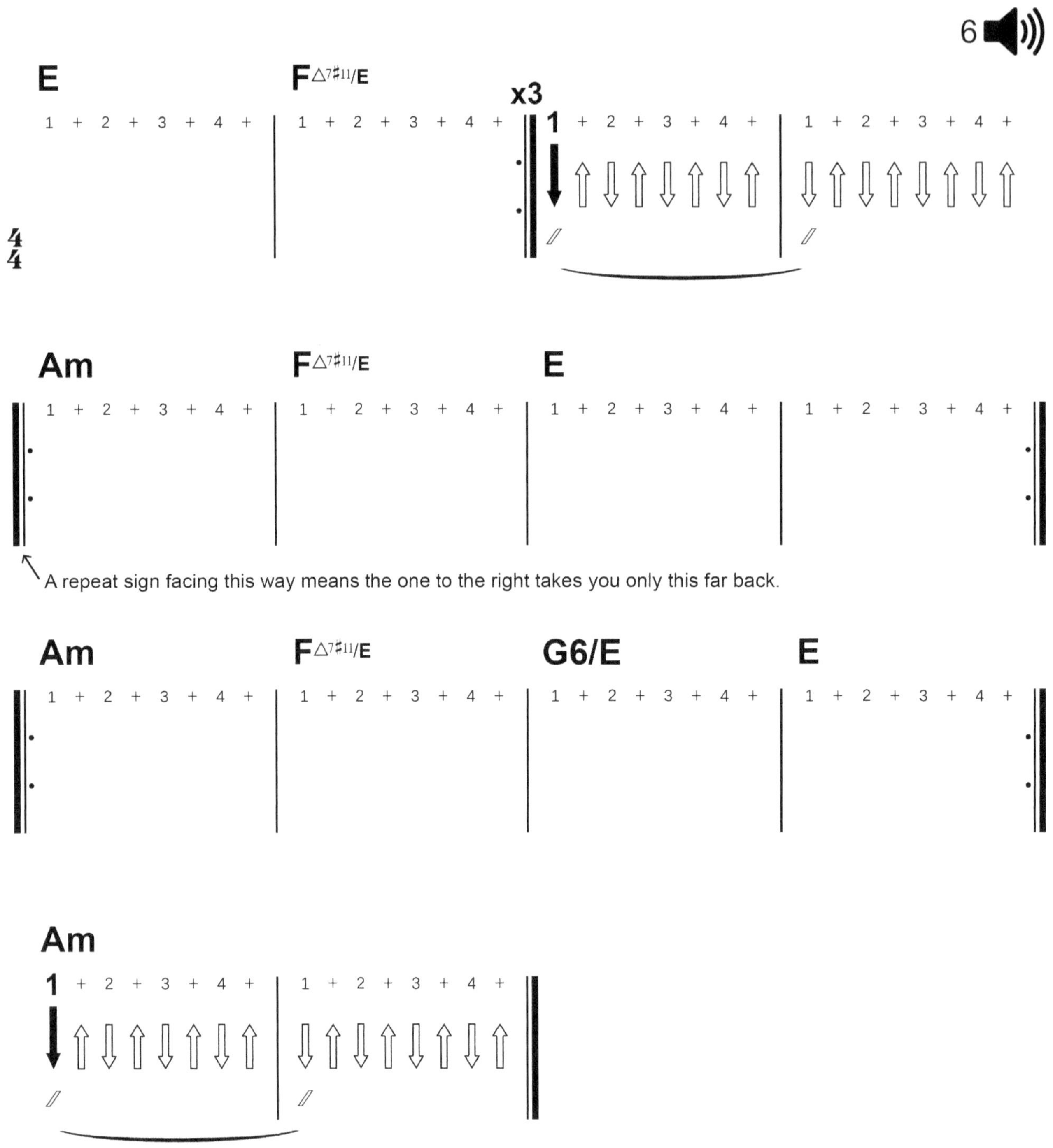

6 🔊))

E   **F$^{\triangle 7\sharp 11}$/E**   **x3**

$\frac{4}{4}$

Am   **F$^{\triangle 7\sharp 11}$/E**   **E**

A repeat sign facing this way means the one to the right takes you only this far back.

Am   **F$^{\triangle 7\sharp 11}$/E**   **G6/E**   **E**

Am

For the next version the first line moves between strumming patterns A18 and C11, the second line moves between patterns A24 and A19 and the third line moves between patterns A23 and C12.

7

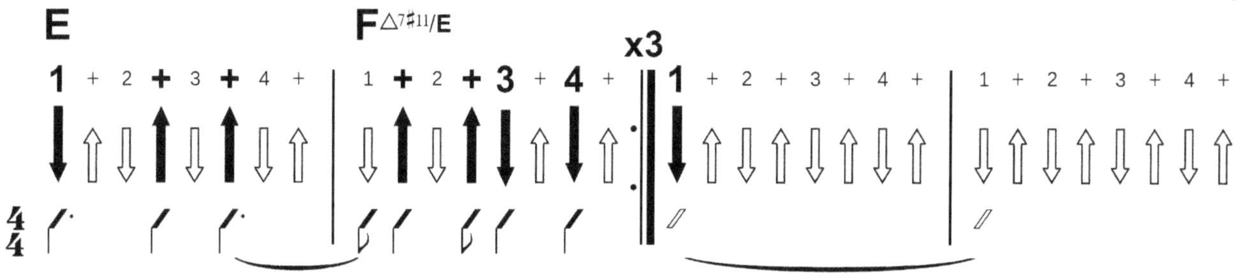
E
F△7♯11/E
x3

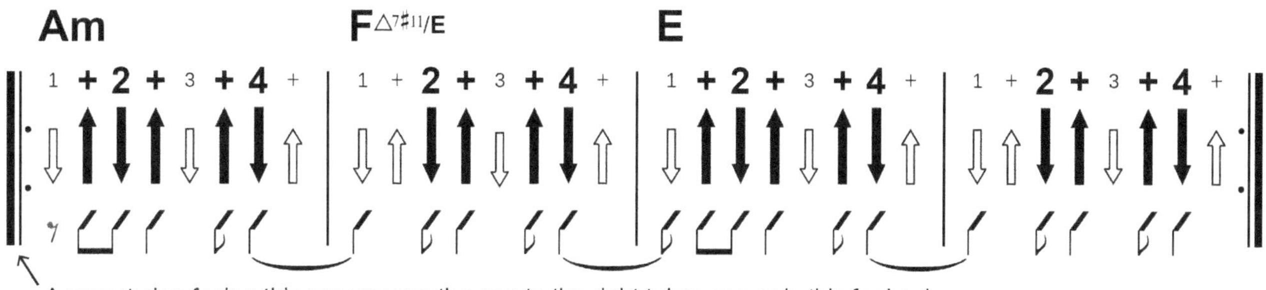
Am
F△7♯11/E
E

A repeat sign facing this way means the one to the right takes you only this far back.

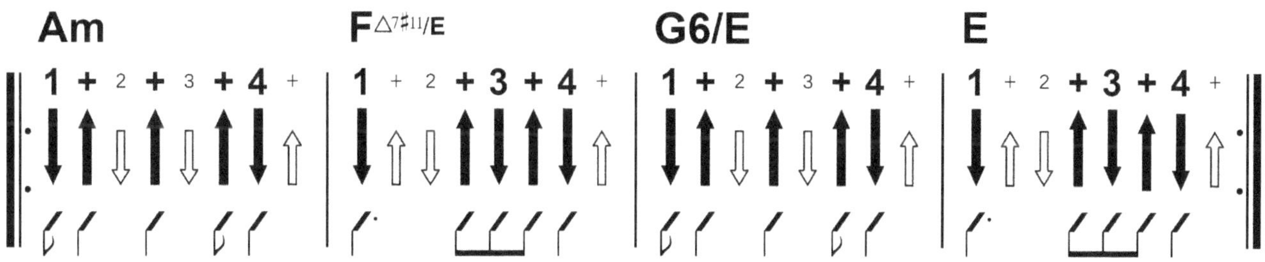
Am
F△7♯11/E
G6/E
E

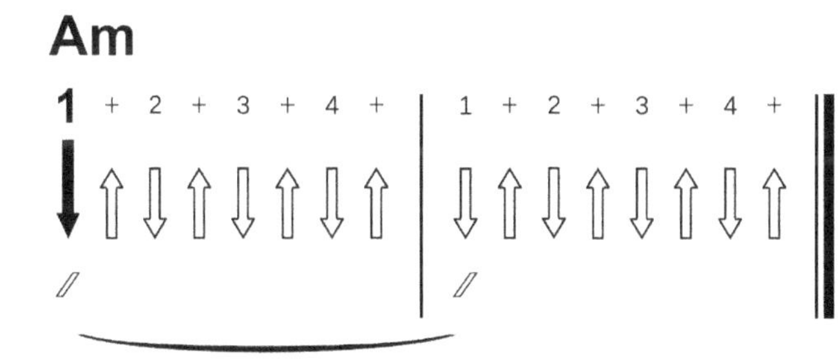
Am

Strumming Exercises 3b

2 Chords per Bar

1

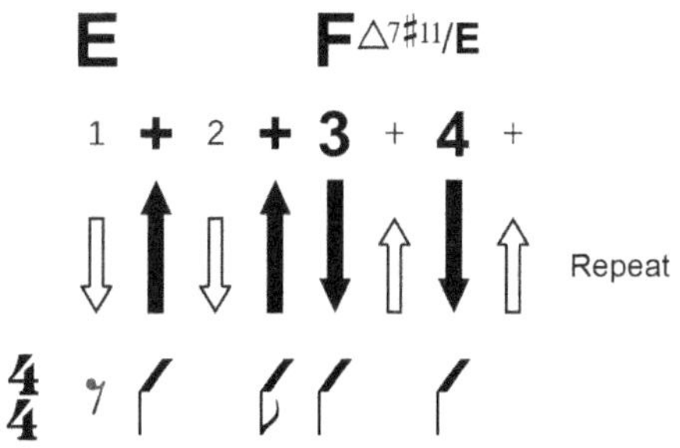
E
F△7♯11/E
Repeat

(Strumming Pattern C11)

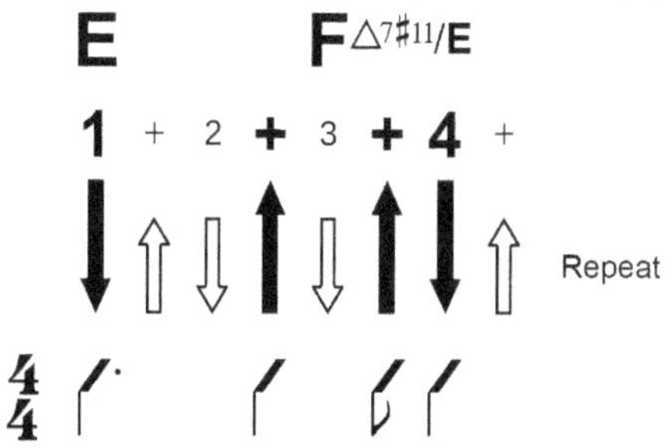
E
F△7♯11/E
Repeat

(Strumming Pattern A16)

Am   **F**$^{\triangle7\sharp11}$**/E**

1 + **2** + 3 **+ 4 +**

(Strumming Pattern A25)

Am   **F**$^{\triangle7\sharp11}$**/E**

1 + **2** + **3 + 4** +

2 🔊

(Strumming Pattern A7)

E   **Am**

1 + 2 + 3 **+ 4** +

(Strumming Pattern A27)

E   **Am**

1 **+ 2** + **3** + **4** +

3 🔊

(Strumming Pattern A11)

F$^{\triangle7\sharp11}$**/E**   **G6/E**

1 + 2 **+** 3 **+ 4** +

(Strumming Pattern A23)

F$^{\triangle7\sharp11}$**/E**   **G6/E**

1 **+ 2 +** 3 + **4** +

4 🔊

(Strumming Pattern A21)

G6/E   **E**

1 + 2 **+ 3 + 4** +

(Strumming Pattern C12)

G6/E   **E**

1 + 2 + **3 +** 4 +

5 🔊

(Strumming Pattern A22)

Study Piece 3b

1 & 2 Chords per Bar

The next piece contains two chords in some of its bars. Choose your own pair of strumming patterns to go back and forth between them for the entire piece. If you would like a demonstration of moving between two strumming patterns in a piece, which has two chords in some of its bars, you could read / listen to the piece after this one, which has its patterns filled in. The strumming pattern(s) you could choose here can be from Patterns A (page 18), B (page 36) or C (page 43).

6 🔊

E | **F△7♯11/E** | **x3** | | |

1 + 2 + 3 + 4 + | 1 + 2 + 3 + 4 + | 1 + 2 + 3 + 4 + | 1 + 2 + 3 + 4 +

4/4

Am | **F△7♯11/E** **E** | **F△7♯11/E** **E**

1 + 2 + 3 + 4 + | 1 + 2 + 3 + 4 + | 1 + 2 + 3 + 4 + | 1 + 2 + 3 + 4 +

Am | **F△7♯11/E** **G6/E** | **E**

1 + 2 + 3 + 4 + | 1 + 2 + 3 + 4 + | 1 + 2 + 3 + 4 + | 1 + 2 + 3 + 4 +

Am

1 + 2 + 3 + 4 + | 1 + 2 + 3 + 4 +

Like the last piece the strumming patterns for this also come in pairs and go back and forth between the two. The first line moves between strumming patterns A18 and C11, the second line moves between patterns A27 and A25 and the third line moves between patterns A23 and C12.

Chord Changes Part V

Relocating all Fretting Fingers

Previously we looked at chord changes in which all the fretting fingers keep the same formation while relocating, due to the chords sharing the same shape. Next we'll look at chord changes in which the fretting fingers need to relocate in different directions, as the chords do not share the same shape.

At first this can be tricky because for most activities the fingers do not work independently to such an extent; they tend to be somewhat "wired" together coordination-wise. For example holding a steering wheel, using a remote control, scratching your head, eating with a knife and fork or holding most kinds of sports equipment / racquet. An exception would be touch-typing so if you can do that you might be at an advantage. That said, the previous chord changes we have studied should put you in a stronger position to deal with this.

The majority of the following chord changes require relocation of all fretting fingers. It is important for the fingers to go directly, in a more or less straight line, to where they are required for the next chord. Anything else by comparison is an inefficient waste of movement. The video example demonstrates this with three of the following chord changes (E to A, G to C and G7 to D). Try to apply this to all of the chord changes.

17 ▶

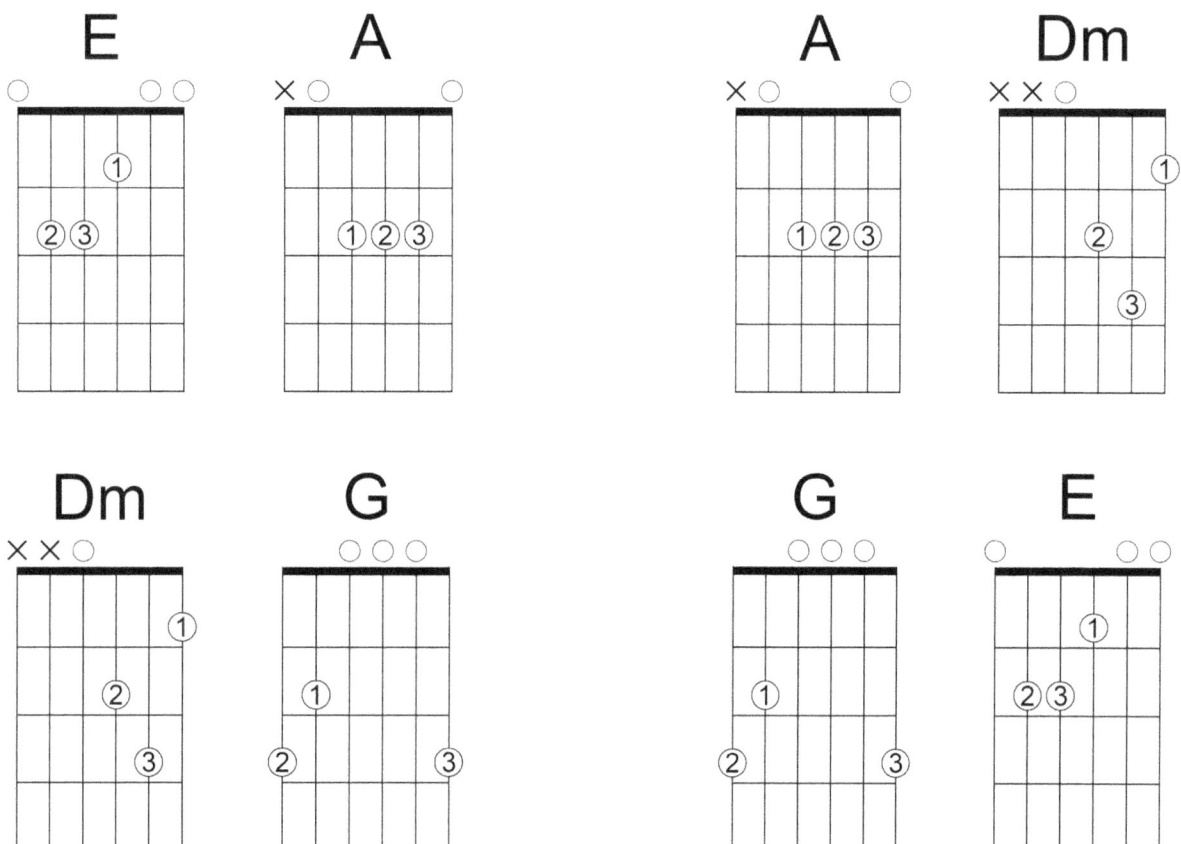

G
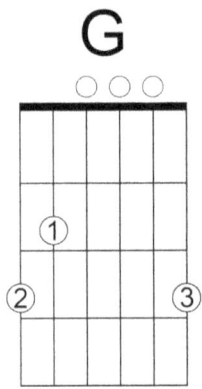

C
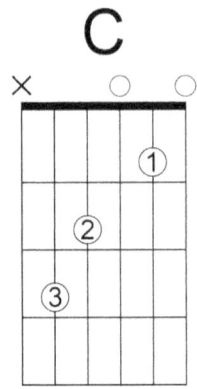

C
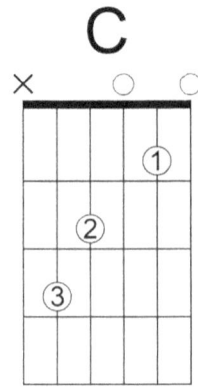

Fmaj7
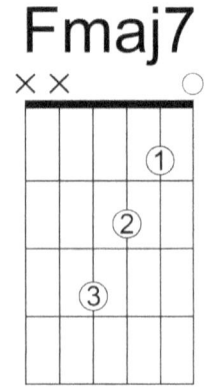

G
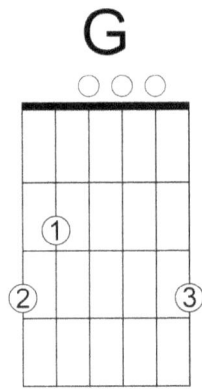

A
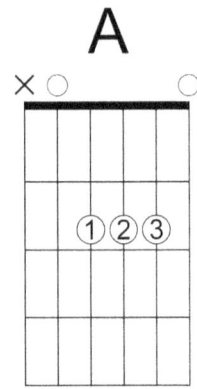

A
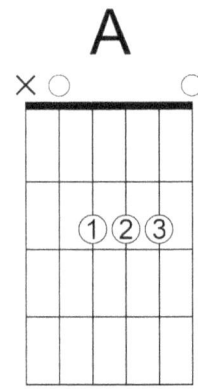

G7
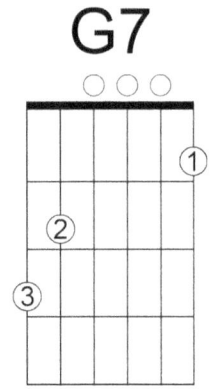

G7
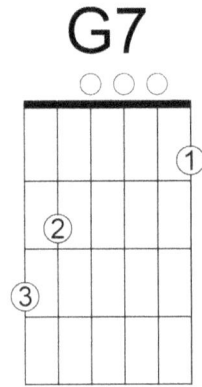

D
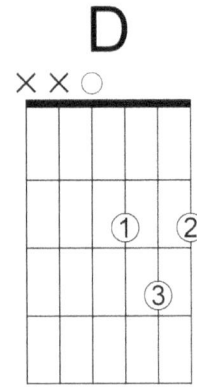

D
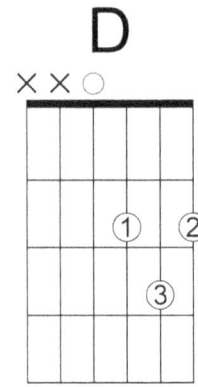

G
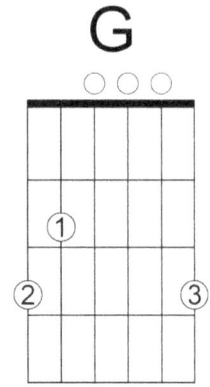

D
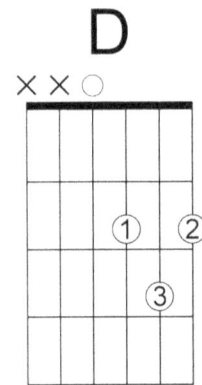

C
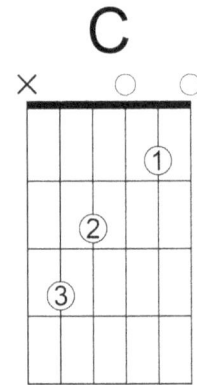

C
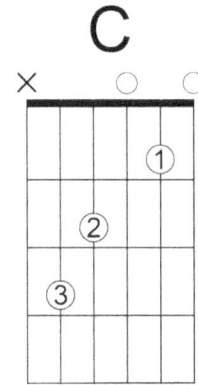

E
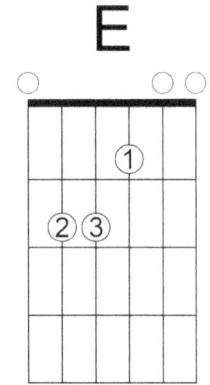

Tip: A tendency for some learners on some of the trickier chord changes is for the fretting fingers to group together before moving to the next chord. This inefficient way of doing it is demonstrated on the video between the chords of G and C (the correct way being on the previous video 17). This will be due to the fingers not being familiar with moving independently from each other, as previously mentioned. As with most things, this can be helped by changing chords slowly at first. It can help to moderately tense your hand and fingers while you do so in order to hold everything in place. The better you get the more your brain learns to use only the muscles that are needed.

18 ▶

It can be worth practising the above chord change pairs with the simple strumming patterns A1 and A2 over the counting audio tracks 1+2+3+4+ or a metronome. Strumming pattern A1 is simply strumming on beats 1 and 3 while A2 is strumming on beats 1, 2, 3 and 4.

Note: For these chord changes in particular (in fact for any chord changes that require relocation of all fretting fingers) it is worth reiterating the earlier comparison to the backstage of a theatre (page 29); there are things you don't see or hear that contribute to what you do see and hear. The process of changing from one chord to the next may not be audible but its importance should not be overlooked for a learner.

Strumming Exercises 4a

1 Chord per Bar

Here are some strumming exercises to try with our new Chord Changes Part V.

1 🔊

(Strumming Pattern A16)

(Strumming Pattern A15)

2 🔊

(Strumming Pattern A5)

(Strumming Pattern A6)

Dm   **G**

(Strumming Pattern A7)

Dm   **G**

(Strumming Pattern A8)

G   **E**

(Strumming Pattern A11)

G   **E**

(Strumming Pattern A22)

G   **C**

(Strumming Pattern A9)

G   **C**

(Strumming Pattern A12)

C   **Fmaj7**

(Strumming Pattern A21)

C   **Fmaj7**

(Strumming Pattern A16)

G   **A**

(Strumming Pattern A23)

G   **A**

(Strumming Pattern A3)

A   **G7**

(Strumming Pattern A7)

A   **G7**

(Strumming Pattern C16)

G7   **D**

(Strumming Pattern C3)

G7   **D**

(Strumming Pattern A25)

D   **G**

(Strumming Pattern A27)

D   **G**

(Strumming Pattern A4)

D   **C**

(Strumming Pattern C11)

D   **C**

(Strumming Pattern C14)

C   **E**

(Strumming Pattern A8)

C   **E**

(Strumming Pattern A26)

Study Piece 4a

1 Chord per Bar

A piece using Chord Changes Part V. Use any patterns from Strumming Patterns A (page 18) or C (page 43); either the same pattern for all the missing bars or two or more patterns.

13 🔊

E	A	Dm	G
1 + 2 + 3 + 4 +	1 + 2 + 3 + 4 +	1 + 2 + 3 + 4 +	1 + 2 + 3 + 4 +

$\frac{4}{4}$

C	Fmaj7	C	G
1 + 2 + 3 + 4 +	1 + 2 + 3 + 4 +	1 + 2 + 3 + 4 +	1 + 2 + 3 + 4 +

A	G7	D	
1 + 2 + 3 + 4 +	1 + 2 + 3 + 4 +	1 + 2 + 3 + 4 +	1 + 2 + 3 + 4 +

D	G	D	
1 + 2 + 3 + 4 +	1 + 2 + 3 + 4 +	1 + 2 + 3 + 4 +	1 + 2 + 3 + 4 +

C	E	A	
1 + 2 + 3 + 4 +	1 + 2 + 3 + 4 +	1 + 2 + 3 + 4 +	**1** + 2 + 3 + 4 +

The following more challenging example has a different strumming pattern for each line. The first line uses strumming pattern A16, the second line uses pattern A21, the third line uses pattern A7, the fourth line uses pattern A27 and the last line uses pattern A8.

Chord Changes Part VI

Relocating all Fretting Fingers

Although this part is titled "Chord Changes", from now on, new chords will be shown on their own rather than in pairs. Hopefully by now, you have enough experience to not need as much guidance. By implication of the title however, you can practise changing between these chords generally. The actual chord changes required for the upcoming study piece are in the following Strumming Exercises 4b, so you could isolate those chord changes to the same effect, i.e. moving between the chords in your own time while strumming each only once, in order to the practise the chord changes on their own.

These chords are extended versions of the previous ones (from Chord Changes Part V) and are therefore often similar in shape. Remember that it is important for the fingers to go directly, in a more or less straight line, to where they are required for the next chord. The video demonstrates three examples (Emaj7 to Amaj7, Gsus4 to Emaj7 and Amaj7 to G7).

19 ▶

Emaj7   Amaj7   Dm7   Gsus4   or   Gsus4

Cmaj7   Fmaj7   G7   D7   E7

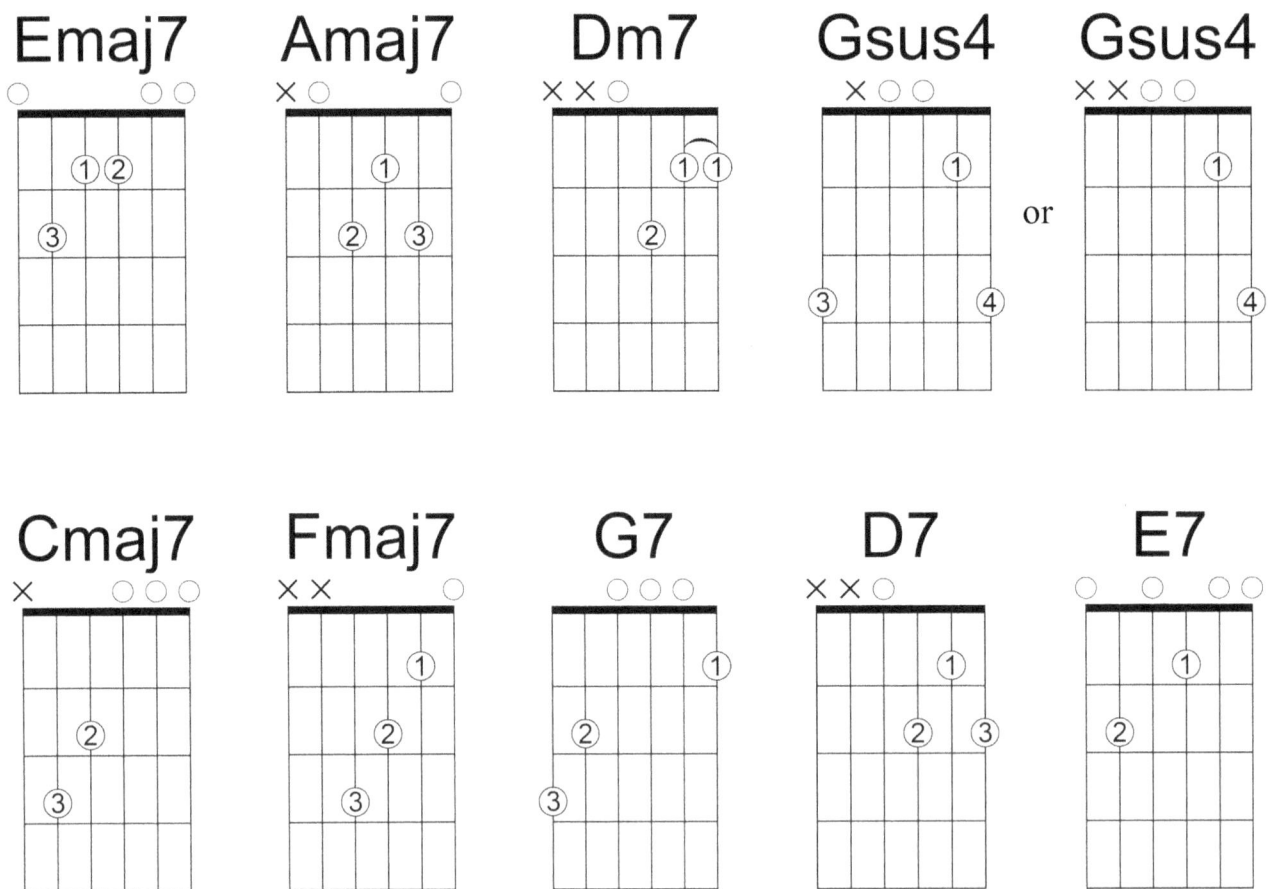

It can be worth practising the chord changes with the simple strumming patterns A1 and A2 over the counting audio tracks 1+2+3+4+ or a metronome. Strumming pattern A1 is simply strumming on beats 1 and 3 while A2 is strumming on beats 1, 2, 3 and 4.

Strumming Exercises 4b

2 Chords per Bar

Here are a few strumming exercises in which there are two chords per bar. The new chords (from Chord Changes Part VI) are used, while the earlier ones (from Chord Changes Part V) are also shown above so you can use either chord sequence. Don't forget when trying these for yourself, they could be played with the counting audio tracks 1+2+3+4+ at various speeds, or while counting for yourself, or over a metronome.

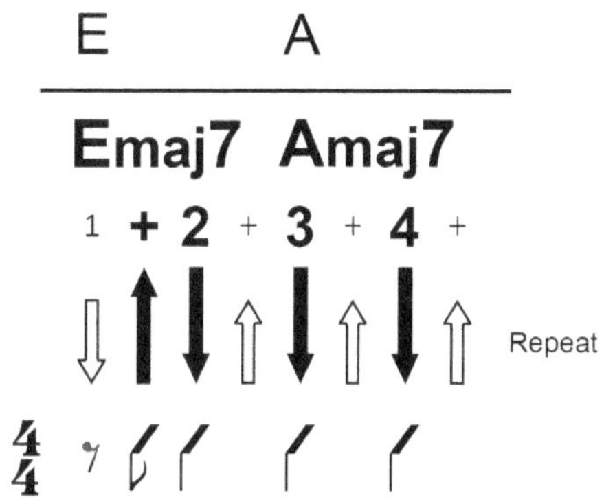

(Strumming Pattern A11)

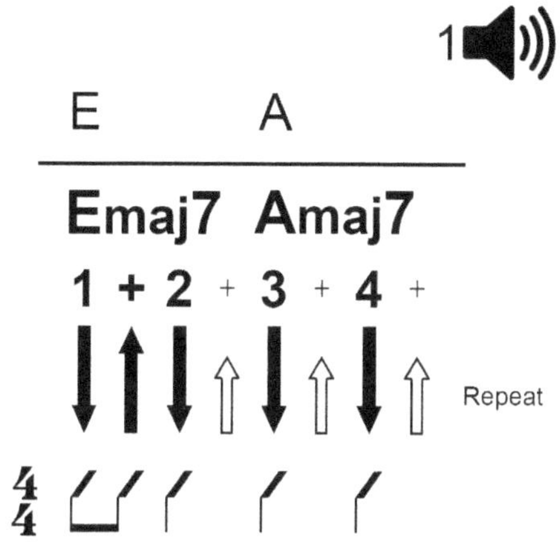

(Strumming Pattern A13)

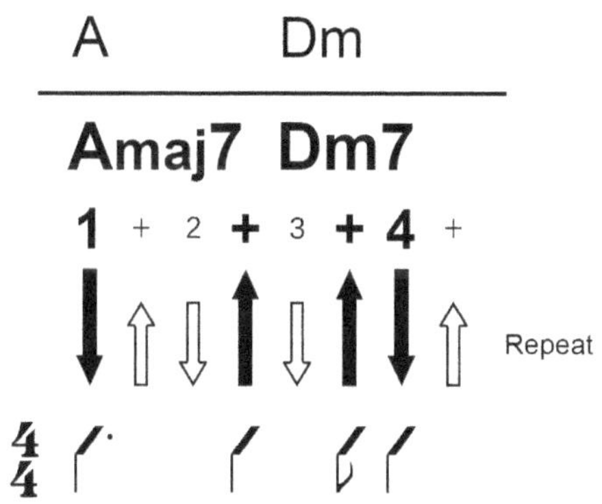

(Strumming Pattern A16)

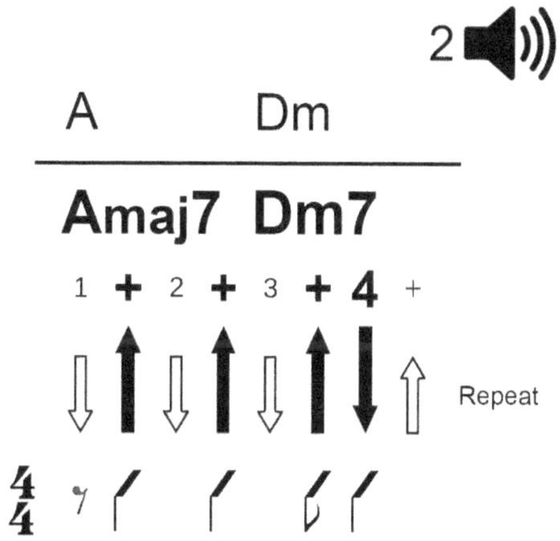

(Strumming Pattern A28)

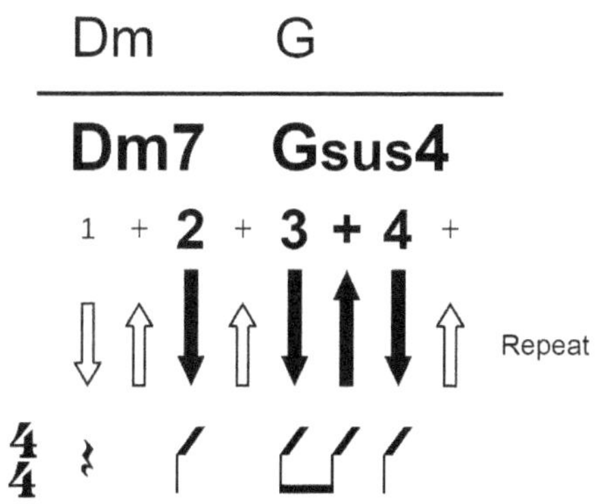

(Strumming Pattern A14)

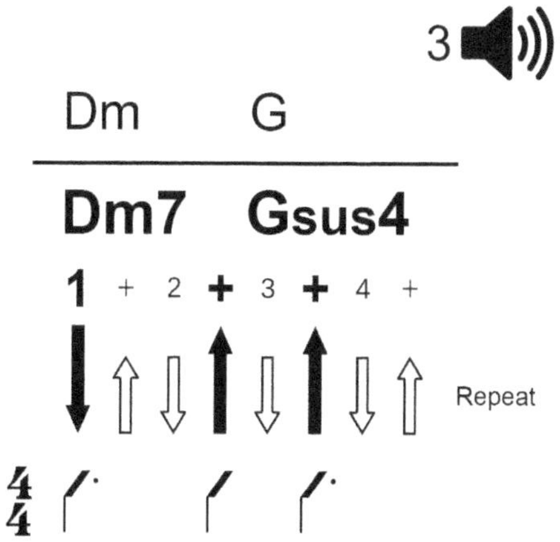

(Strumming Pattern A18)

G   E

Gsus4 Emaj7

1 + 2 + 3 **+ 4** +

(Strumming Pattern A27)

G   E

Gsus4 Emaj7

1 + 2 + **3** + **4** +

Repeat

(Strumming Pattern A13)

G   C

Gsus4 Cmaj7

1 + **2 +** 3 **+ 4** +

Repeat

(Strumming Pattern A19)

G   C

Gsus4 Cmaj7

1 **+ 2** + **3 + 4** +

Repeat

(Strumming Pattern A20)

C   Fmaj7

Cmaj7 Fmaj7

1 **+ 2 + 3** + **4** +

Repeat

(Strumming Pattern A21)

C   Fmaj7

Cmaj7 Fmaj7

1 **+ 2 +** 3 **+ 4** +

Repeat

(Strumming Pattern A24)

G   A

Gsus4 Amaj7

1 **+** 2 **+** 3 **+ 4** +

$\frac{4}{4}$ Repeat

(Strumming Pattern A28)

G   A

Gsus4 Amaj7

1 + **2** + 3 **+ 4** +

$\frac{4}{4}$ Repeat

(Strumming Pattern A10)

A   G7

Amaj7 G7

1 + **2** + **3 + 4** +

$\frac{4}{4}$ Repeat

(Strumming Pattern A7)

A   G7

Amaj7 G7

1 + 2 + **3** + **4** +

$\frac{4}{4}$ Repeat

(Strumming Pattern A3)

G7   D

G7   D7

1 + **2 +** 3 + **4** +

$\frac{4}{4}$ Repeat

(Strumming Pattern A4)

G7   D

G7   D7

1 + **2** + **3 +** 4 +

$\frac{4}{4}$ Repeat

(Strumming Pattern A5)

10 🔊

D   C

D7   **Cmaj7**

1 + **2** + **3** + **4** **+**

Repeat

4/4

(Strumming Pattern A6)

D   C

D7   **Cmaj7**

1 + **2** + 3 **+** 4 +

Repeat

4/4

(Strumming Pattern A9)

11 🔊

C   E

Cmaj7 E7

1 + **2** + 3 **+** **4** +

Repeat

4/4

(Strumming Pattern A8)

C   E

Cmaj7 E7

1 + **2** + 3 **+** **4** +

Repeat

4/4

(Strumming Pattern A10)

12 🔊

E   A

E7   **Amaj7**

1 **+** 2 **+** 3 **+** 4 +

Repeat

4/4

(Strumming Pattern A26)

E   A

E7   **Amaj7**

1 **+** **2** + **3** **+** **4** +

Repeat

4/4

(Strumming Pattern A20)

Study Piece 4b

1 & 2 Chords per Bar

For the following study piece the new chords (from Chord Changes Part VI) are shown in the usual place above the bars. The previous chords (from Chord Changes Part V) are also included in brackets above the new chords. Both sets of chords will work over the same backing track.

Use any patterns from Strumming Patterns A (page 18). As before you could use the same strumming pattern for all of the missing bars. A little trickier would be two different patterns, such as one strumming pattern for lines one and two, then another strumming pattern for lines three and four.

13 🔊

(E)	(A)	(Dm)	(G)
Emaj7	Amaj7	Dm7	Gsus4
1 + 2 + 3 + 4 +	1 + 2 + 3 + 4 +	1 + 2 + 3 + 4 +	1 + 2 + 3 + 4 +

4/4

(C)	(Fmaj7)	(C)	(G)	(A)		(G7)
Cmaj7	Fmaj7	Cmaj7	Gsus4	Amaj7		G7
1 + 2 + 3 + 4 +	1 + 2 + 3 + 4 +	1 + 2 + 3 + 4 +	1 + 2 + 3 + 4 +

(D)		(D)	(G)	(D)
D7		D7	G7	D7
1 + 2 + 3 + 4 +	1 + 2 + 3 + 4 +	1 + 2 + 3 + 4 +	1 + 2 + 3 + 4 +

(C)	(E)	(A)	
Cmaj7	E7	Amaj7	
1 + 2 + 3 + 4 +	1 + 2 + 3 + 4 +	1 + 2 + 3 + 4 +	1 + 2 + 3 + 4 +

71

The following example, which you may find more challenging, has several different strumming patterns. The first line uses strumming pattern A16, the second line uses patterns A21 then A13, the third line uses pattern A13 then A27 and the last line uses pattern A24.

14 🔊))

Chord Changes Part VII

Relocating all Fretting Fingers

The final set of chord changes. Changing between most of these will require relocation of all used fretting fingers. The video demonstrates three examples; E6 to Aadd9, Dmaj7 to Fadd9 and Dm7 to Esus4. Where the Dmaj7 chord features on the video, it is also shown with another optional fingering.

20 ▶

D6   E6   Aadd9   Asus2   *Dmaj7

or

Tip: If you find Aadd9 too challenging you could use Asus2 for a while instead as the two chords are functionally very similar.

*Dmaj7   Fadd9   G7   Am   G6

C   Dm7   Esus4   E   A

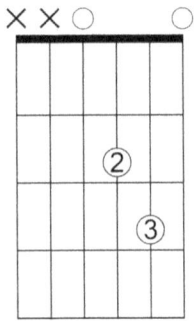
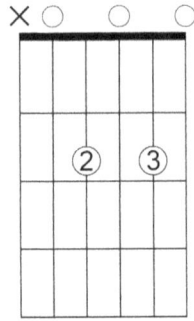
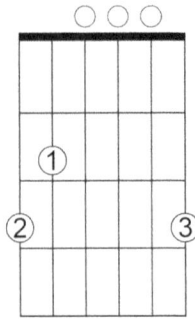

Dsus2 A7 G

* The chord of Dmaj7 is shown with two optional fingerings.

Open Strums

Not only are the above chord changes the most advanced so far, but we are also soon to change between them over eighth notes. Due to this, now is a good time to explain open strums. Open strums fulfil a similar purpose to the earlier mentioned pre-emptive chord changing (page 23), in that they make things easier for the fretting hand, while not significantly changing the structure of the music.

As implied by the name, an open strum is to strum the strings open. In other words to strum while the fretting hand does not press down on any of the frets, leaving it temporarily free, thereby allowing a bit more time for it to change to the next chord. The following two examples are taken from the forthcoming "Strumming Exercises 5a" and include video demonstrations at 80bpm. First changing between D6 and E6.

21 ▶

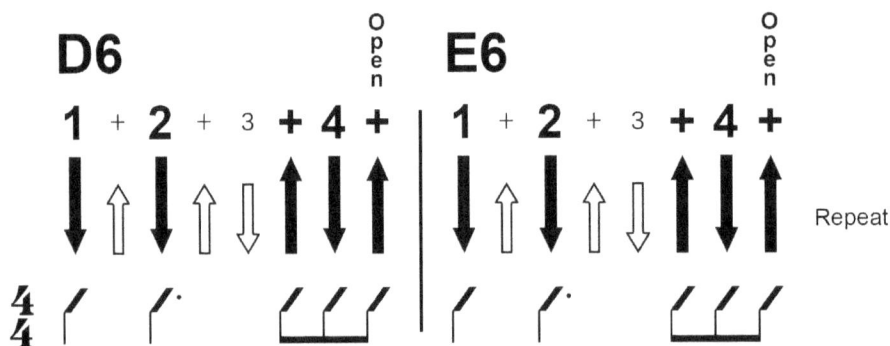

Here's another example, changing between E6 and Aadd9.

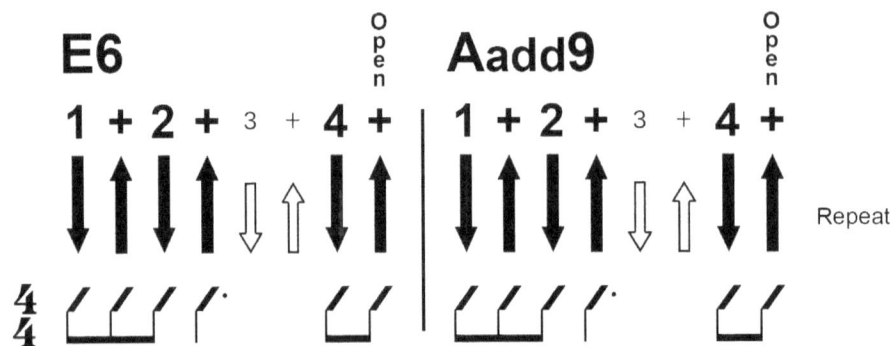

Open strums can also be purposefully used for effect, similar to how a singer might briefly break their voice, intentionally or not, to a much higher, out-of-key note, before the next intentional note. An example of a song that uses open strums, would be "What's Up" by the band 4 Non-Blondes. For the strummed acoustic guitar part, before each chord change, a few open strums are played. This is most noticeable at the start of the song. Another example is "Teen Spirit" by the band Nirvana. For the introduction, a solo strummed guitar part is heard, in which some open strums are used.

Open strums can be used wherever there are chord changes between eighth notes. Bear in mind, for chord changes in which fretting finger locations are shared, open strums may defeat the point. For example, even though earlier study pieces 2a and 2b have chord changes between eighth notes, open strums don't serve as much of an advantage. Remember, you don't *have to* use open strums but if it helps you with the chord changes then you can.

Strumming Exercises 5a

1 Chord per Bar

The following exercises require a chord change between eighth notes from one bar to the next. The new chords are used (from Chord Changes Part VII), while previous ones (from Chord Changes VI and V) are also shown above so you have a variety of options.

(Strumming Pattern B6)

(Strumming Pattern B13)

(Strumming Pattern B16)

(Strumming Pattern B18)

Note: Don't forget if Aadd9 is too challenging it can be substituted with Asus2.

3 🔊

Dm	G
Dm7	Gsus4

Aadd9 **Dmaj7**

1 + 2 + 3 + 4 + | 1 + 2 + 3 + 4 +

Repeat

4/4

(Strumming Pattern B21)

Dm	G
Dm7	Gsus4

Aadd9 **Dmaj7**

1 + 2 + 3 + 4 + | 1 + 2 + 3 + 4 +

Repeat

4/4

(Strumming Pattern B3)

4 🔊

G	E
Gsus4	Emaj7

Dmaj7 **D6**

1 + 2 + 3 + 4 + | 1 + 2 + 3 + 4 +

Repeat

4/4

(Strumming Pattern B7)

G	E
Gsus4	Emaj7

Dmaj7 **D6**

1 + 2 + 3 + 4 + | 1 + 2 + 3 + 4 +

Repeat

4/4

(Strumming Pattern B10)

5 🔊

G	C
Gsus4	Cmaj7

Dmaj7 **Fadd9**

1 + 2 + 3 + 4 + | 1 + 2 + 3 + 4 +

Repeat

4/4

(Strumming Pattern B19)

G	C
Gsus4	Cmaj7

Dmaj7 **Fadd9**

1 + 2 + 3 + 4 + | 1 + 2 + 3 + 4 +

Repeat

4/4

(Strumming Pattern B22)

6 🔊

C	Fmaj7
Cmaj7	Fmaj7

Fadd9 **G7**

1 + 2 + 3 + 4 + | 1 + 2 + 3 + 4 +

Repeat

4/4

(Strumming Pattern B10)

C	Fmaj7
Cmaj7	Fmaj7

Fadd9 **G7**

1 + 2 + 3 + 4 + | 1 + 2 + 3 + 4 +

Repeat

4/4

(Strumming Pattern B4)

G	E
G7	E
G7	**Am**

1 + 2 + 3 + 4 + | 1 + 2 + 3 + 4 +   Repeat

4/4

(Strumming Pattern B11)

G	E
G7	E
G7	**Am**

1 + 2 + 3 + 4 + | 1 + 2 + 3 + 4 +   Repeat

4/4

(Strumming Pattern B1)

C	G
Cmaj7	Gsus4
Am	**G6**

1 + 2 + 3 + 4 + | 1 + 2 + 3 + 4 +   Repeat

4/4

(Strumming Pattern B17)

C	G
Cmaj7	Gsus4
Am	**G6**

1 + 2 + 3 + 4 + | 1 + 2 + 3 + 4 +   Repeat

4/4

(Strumming Pattern B9)

C	D
Cmaj7	D7
G6	**Fadd9**

1 + 2 + 3 + 4 + | 1 + 2 + 3 + 4 +   Repeat

4/4

(Strumming Pattern B14)

C	D
Cmaj7	D7
G6	**Fadd9**

1 + 2 + 3 + 4 + | 1 + 2 + 3 + 4 +   Repeat

4/4

(Strumming Pattern B8)

G	A
Gsus4	Amaj7
G6	**C**

1 + 2 + 3 + 4 + | 1 + 2 + 3 + 4 +   Repeat

4/4

(Strumming Pattern B7)

G	A
Gsus4	Amaj7
G6	**C**

1 + 2 + 3 + 4 + | 1 + 2 + 3 + 4 +   Repeat

4/4

(Strumming Pattern B14)

A	G7
Amaj7	G7
C	**Dm7**

1 + 2 + 3 + 4 + | 1 + 2 + 3 + 4 + Repeat

4/4

(Strumming Pattern B20)

A	G7
Amaj7	G7
C	**Dm7**

1 + 2 + 3 + 4 + | 1 + 2 + 3 + 4 + Repeat

4/4

(Strumming Pattern B2)

G7	D
G7	D7
Dm7	**Esus4**

1 + 2 + 3 + 4 + | 1 + 2 + 3 + 4 + Repeat

4/4

(Strumming Pattern B5)

G7	D
G7	D7
Dm7	**Esus4**

1 + 2 + 3 + 4 + | 1 + 2 + 3 + 4 + Repeat

4/4

(Strumming Pattern B6)

G7	Am
G6	Fadd9
Esus4	**E**

1 + 2 + 3 + 4 + | 1 + 2 + 3 + 4 + Repeat

4/4

(Strumming Pattern B21)

G7	Am
G6	Fadd9
Esus4	**E**

1 + 2 + 3 + 4 + | 1 + 2 + 3 + 4 + Repeat

4/4

(Strumming Pattern B15)

A	E7
A	A7
A	**Dsus2**

1 + 2 + 3 + 4 + | 1 + 2 + 3 + 4 + Repeat

4/4

(Strumming Pattern B17)

A	E7
A	A7
A	**Dsus2**

1 + 2 + 3 + 4 + | 1 + 2 + 3 + 4 + Repeat

4/4

(Strumming Pattern B16)

D	C
D7	Cmaj7
A7	**Dm7**

1 + 2 **+** 3 **+** 4 **+** | **1** + 2 **+** 3 **+** 4 **+**

4/4

(Strumming Pattern B18)

D	C
D7	Cmaj7
A7	**Dm7**

1 + 2 + 3 **+** 4 **+** | **1 + 2 +** 3 **+** 4 **+**

4/4

(Strumming Pattern B22)

C	E
Cmaj7	E7
Dm7	**G**

1 + 2 + **3** + **4 +** | **1 +** 2 + **3** + **4 +**

4/4

(Strumming Pattern B13)

C	E
Cmaj7	E7
Dm7	**G**

1 + **2** + **3** + 4 **+** | **1** + **2** + **3** + 4 **+**

4/4

(Strumming Pattern B3)

E	A
E7	Amaj7
G	**Am**

1 + **2 +** 3 + **4 +** | **1** + **2 +** 3 + **4 +**

4/4

(Strumming Pattern B4)

E	A
E7	Amaj7
G	**Am**

1 + **2** + **3** + **4 +** | **1** + **2** + **3** + **4 +**

4/4

(Strumming Pattern B1)

79

Study Piece 5a
1 Chord per Bar

With Chord Changes Part VII or VI. Use any strumming patterns from Patterns B (page 36); either the same pattern or two or more.

18&19 🔊))

(Emaj7) **D6**	(Amaj7) **E6**	(Dm7) **Aadd9**	(Gsus4) **Dmaj7**
1 + 2 + 3 + 4 +	1 + 2 + 3 + 4 +	1 + 2 + 3 + 4 +	1 + 2 + 3 + 4 +

$\frac{4}{4}$

(Cmaj7) **Fadd9**	(Fmaj7) **G7**	(Cmaj7) **Am**	(Gsus4) **G6**
1 + 2 + 3 + 4 +	1 + 2 + 3 + 4 +	1 + 2 + 3 + 4 +	1 + 2 + 3 + 4 +

(Amaj7) **C**	(G7) **Dm7**	(D7) **Esus4**	(D7) **E**
1 + 2 + 3 + 4 +	1 + 2 + 3 + 4 +	1 + 2 + 3 + 4 +	1 + 2 + 3 + 4 +

(D7) **A**	(G7) **Dsus2**	(D7) **A**	(D7) **A7**
1 + 2 + 3 + 4 +	1 + 2 + 3 + 4 +	1 + 2 + 3 + 4 +	1 + 2 + 3 + 4 +

(Cmaj7) **Dm7**	(E7) **G**	(Amaj7) **Am**	**1** + 2 + 3 + 4 +
1 + 2 + 3 + 4 +	1 + 2 + 3 + 4 +	1 + 2 + 3 + 4 +	↓

Note: Don't forget that if you find Aadd9 too challenging it can be substituted with Asus2.

The following more challenging version has a different strumming pattern for each line of the piece. The first line uses strumming pattern B6, the second line uses B10, the third line uses B20, the fourth line uses B17 and the last line uses B13.

Strumming Exercises 5b

2 Chords per Bar

The following exercises require a chord change between eighth notes within the same bar. The current chords are used (from Chord Changes Part VII), while previous ones (from Chord Changes VI and V) are also shown above so you have a variety of options.

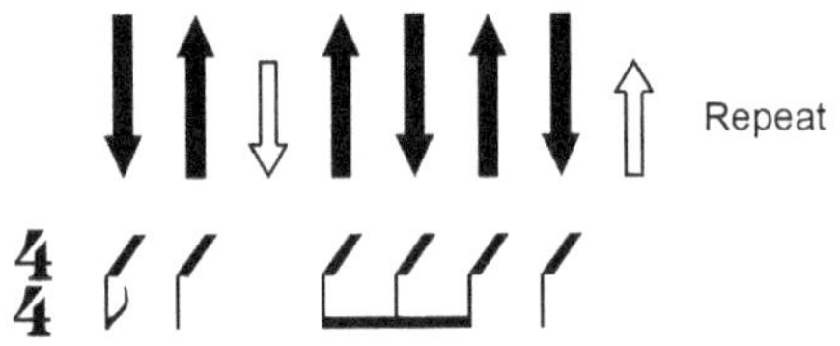

E A

Emaj7 Amaj7

D6 E6

1 + 2 **+ 3 + 4** +

(Strumming Pattern C18)

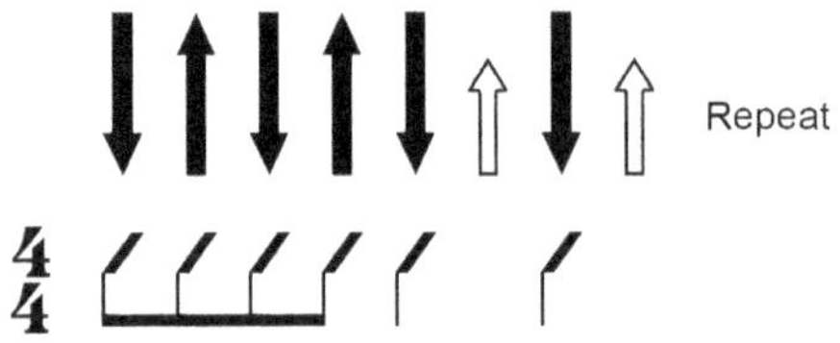

1

E A

Emaj7 Amaj7

D6 E6

1 + 2 + 3 + **4** +

(Strumming Pattern C7)

A Dm

Amaj7 Dm7

E6 Aadd9

1 + 2 **+ 3 +** 4 +

(Strumming Pattern C4)

2

A Dm

Amaj7 Dm7

E6 Aadd9

1 + 2 + 3 + 4 **+**

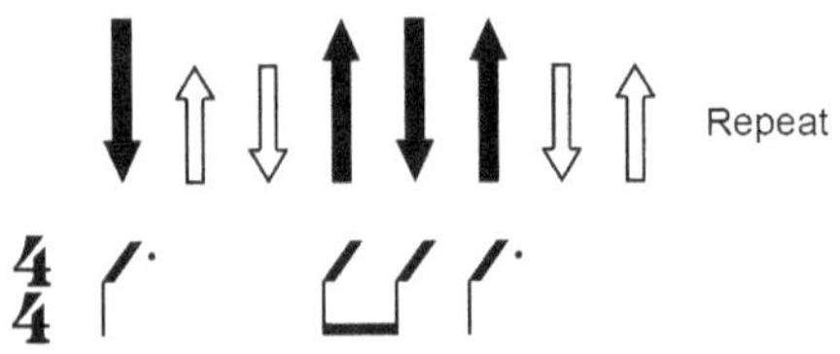

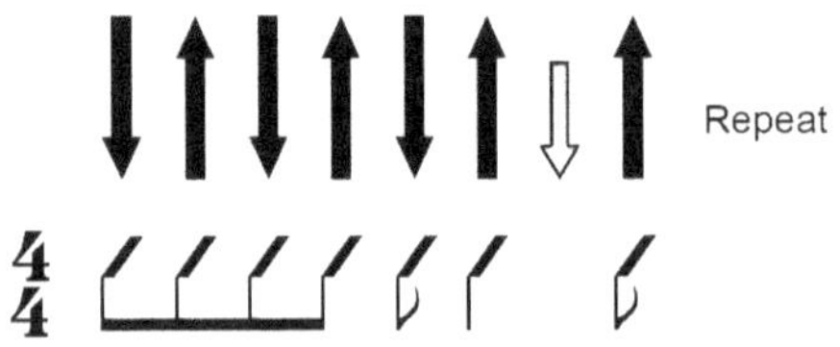

(Strumming Pattern C20)

Dm	G
Dm	Gsus4

Aadd9 Dmaj7

1 **+ 2 + 3** + **4** +

$\frac{4}{4}$ (Strumming Pattern C5)

Dm	G
Dm	Gsus4

Aadd9 Dmaj7

1 + 2 **+ 3 +** 4 +

$\frac{4}{4}$ (Strumming Pattern C14)

G	E
Gsus4	Emaj7

Dmaj7 D6

1 + 2 + 3 + **4** +

$\frac{4}{4}$ (Strumming Pattern C7)

G	E
Gsus4	Emaj7

Dmaj7 D6

1 **+** 2 **+ 3** + **4 +**

$\frac{4}{4}$ (Strumming Pattern C15)

G	C
Gsus4	Cmaj7

Dmaj7 Fadd9

1 + **2 + 3 + 4** +

$\frac{4}{4}$ (Strumming Pattern C10)

G	C
Gsus4	Cmaj7

Dmaj7 Fadd9

1 + **2 + 3** + 4 **+**

$\frac{4}{4}$ (Strumming Pattern C9)

C	Fmaj7
Cmaj7	Fmaj7

Fadd9 G7

1 + 2 + 3 + 4 +

(Strumming Pattern C8)

C	Fmaj7
Cmaj7	Fmaj7

Fadd9 G7

1 + 2 + 3 + 4 +

Repeat

(Strumming Pattern C3)

G	E
G7	E

G7 Am

1 + 2 + 3 + 4 +

Repeat

(Strumming Pattern C20)

G	E
G7	E

G7 Am

1 + 2 + 3 + 4 +

Repeat

(Strumming Pattern C4)

C	G
Cmaj7	Gsus4

Am G6

1 + 2 + 3 + 4 +

Repeat

(Strumming Pattern C18)

C	G
Cmaj7	Gsus4

Am G6

1 + 2 + 3 + 4 +

Repeat

(Strumming Pattern C6)

G A

Gsus4 Amaj7

G6 C

1 + 2 + 3 + 4 +

Repeat

4/4

(Strumming Pattern C1)

G A

Gsus4 Amaj7

G6 C

1 + 2 + 3 + 4 +

Repeat

4/4

(Strumming Pattern C10)

A G7

Amaj7 G7

C Dm7

1 + 2 + 3 + 4 +

Repeat

4/4

(Strumming Pattern C6)

10

A G7

Amaj7 G7

C Dm7

1 + 2 + 3 + 4 +

Repeat

4/4

(Strumming Pattern C5)

G7 D

G7 D7

Dm7 Esus4

1 + 2 + 3 + 4 +

Repeat

4/4

(Strumming Pattern C19)

11

G7 D

G7 D7

Dm7 Esus4

1 + 2 + 3 + 4 +

Repeat

4/4

(Strumming Pattern C8)

G7	Am
G6	Fadd9

Esus4 E

1 + 2 + 3 + 4 +

4/4

Repeat

(Strumming Pattern C5)

G7	Am
G6	Fadd9

Esus4 E

1 + 2 + 3 + 4 +

4/4

Repeat

(Strumming Pattern C18)

A	E7
A	A7

A   Dsus2

1 + 2 + 3 + 4 +

4/4

Repeat

(Strumming Pattern C17)

A	E7
A	A7

A   Dsus2

1 + 2 + 3 + 4 +

4/4

Repeat

(Strumming Pattern C7)

D	C
D7	Cmaj7

A7   Dm7

1 + 2 + 3 + 4 +

4/4

Repeat

(Strumming Pattern C2)

D	C
D7	Cmaj7

A7   Dm7

1 + 2 + 3 + 4 +

4/4

Repeat

(Strumming Pattern C13)

C	E
Cmaj7	E7
Dm7	**G**

1 + 2 + 3 + 4 +

↓↑ ⇑ ↑↑ ⇑ ↓ ⇑ Repeat

$\frac{4}{4}$

(Strumming Pattern C3)

C	E
Cmaj7	E7
Dm7	**G**

1 + 2 + 3 + 4 +

↓↑ ⇑ ↑↓↑ ⇑ ↑ Repeat

$\frac{4}{4}$

(Strumming Pattern C19)

E	A
E7	Amaj7
G	**Am**

1 + 2 + 3 + 4 +

↓ ⇑ ↓↑↑↓ ↓ ⇑ Repeat

$\frac{4}{4}$

(Strumming Pattern C10)

E	A
E7	Amaj7
G	**Am**

1 + 2 + 3 + 4 +

↓ ⇑ ⇑ ↑↓↑↓ ⇑ Repeat

$\frac{4}{4}$

(Strumming Pattern C12)

Study Piece 5b

1 & 2 Chords per Bar

A piece with Chord Changes Part VII or VI and some bars containing two chords. Use any strumming patterns from Patterns C (page 43); either the same pattern for all of the missing bars or two or more.

17&18 🔊))

(Emaj7) (Amaj7) (Dm7) (Gsus4)
D6   **E6**   **Aadd9** **Dmaj7**

1 + 2 + 3 + 4 +   1 + 2 + 3 + 4 +   1 + 2 + 3 + 4 +   1 + 2 + 3 + 4 +

$\frac{4}{4}$

(Cmaj7) (Fmaj7) (Cmaj7) (Gsus4) (Amaj7)   (G7)
Fadd9 G7   **Am   G6**   **C**   **Dm7**

1 + 2 + 3 + 4 +   1 + 2 + 3 + 4 +   1 + 2 + 3 + 4 +   1 + 2 + 3 + 4 +

(D7)   (D7)   (D7) (G7)   (D7)   (D7)
Esus4   **E**   **A** **Dsus2** **A**   **A7**

1 + 2 + 3 + 4 +   1 + 2 + 3 + 4 +   1 + 2 + 3 + 4 +   1 + 2 + 3 + 4 +

(Cmaj7) (E7) (Amaj7)
Dm7   G   **Am**

1 + 2 + 3 + 4 +   1 + 2 + 3 + 4 +   1 + 2 + 3 + 4 +   **1** + 2 + 3 + 4 +

The following more challenging version has several strumming patterns. The first line uses strumming pattern C18, the second line uses pattern C8 then C6, the third line continues with pattern C6 for its first two bars then uses C17 for its latter two bars and the last line uses pattern C3.

19 🔊))

Summary

Here's a summary of what we should now be accustomed to.

- Chord changes requiring relocation of the fretting fingers with the same shape (Chord Changes Part IV), one chord per bar (3a) and two chords per bar (3b) and Alternating Strumming Patterns (3a and 3b).

- Chord changes, between quarter notes, requiring relocation of the fretting fingers with different shapes, meaning the fretting fingers need to move in independent directions (Chord Changes Parts V and VI), one chord per bar (4a) and two chords per bar (4b).

- Open Strums, which can help with chord changes between eighth notes.

- Chord changes, between eighth notes, requiring relocation of the fretting fingers with different shapes, meaning the fretting fingers need to move in different directions, (Chord Changes Parts VII), one chord per bar (5a) and two chords per bar (5b).

For Audio and Video please go to:

www.intuition-books.com

(The reason the link to the audio & video is at the back is so that it is only viewable to people who have bought a copy and to keep the bandwidth reserved for you)

All music written, performed and recorded by Gareth Evans. Backing tracks made using Session Band by UK Music Apps Ltd. Real Band by PG Music Inc. and Superior Drummer by ToonTrack.

Are you ready for Book 2? In the second book for intermediate level and above, you can learn about strumming power chords, strumming in 3/4 time, barre chords, swing feel, early chord changes, using a capo to change key, using a capo to avoid barre chords, muted strums and 16th note strumming in 6/8 time and 4/4 time.

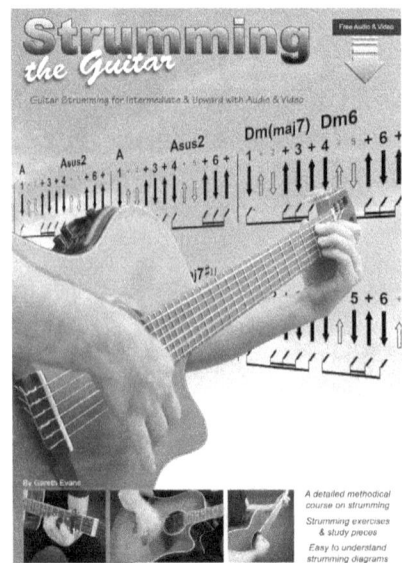

Also available…

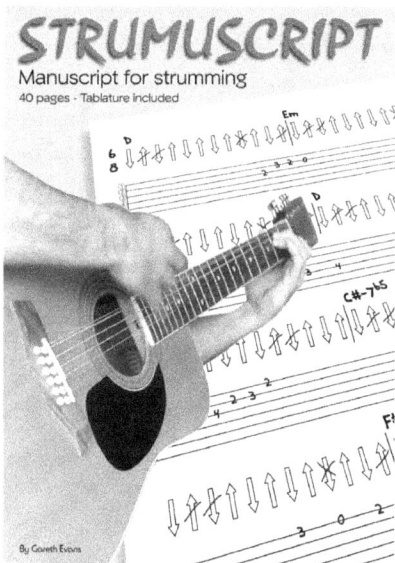

Write down your strumming patterns with Strumuscript

Over 200 movable shapes based on the CAGED system for over 60 types of chord

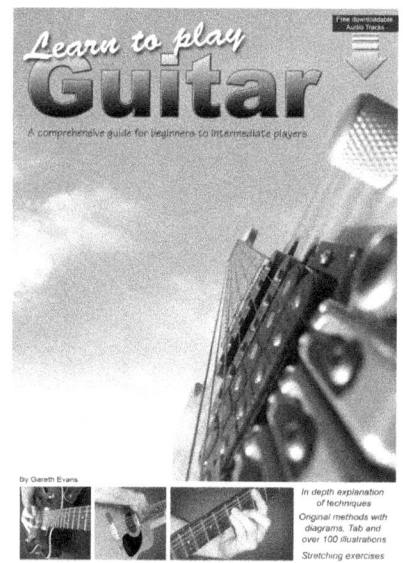

Learn to Play Guitar. A comprehensive guide

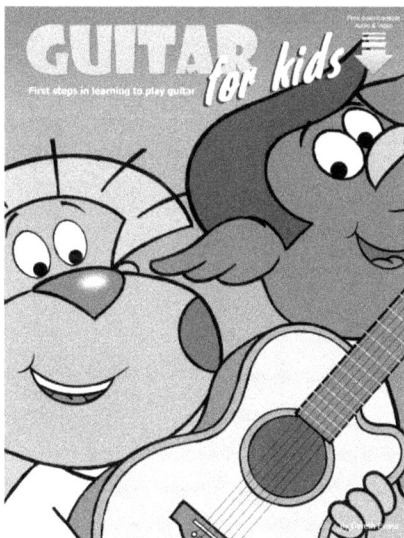

A book for kids on the first steps in learning to play

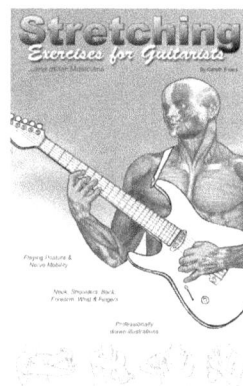

A compact 32 page stretching guide to be used as part of a healthy practise regime

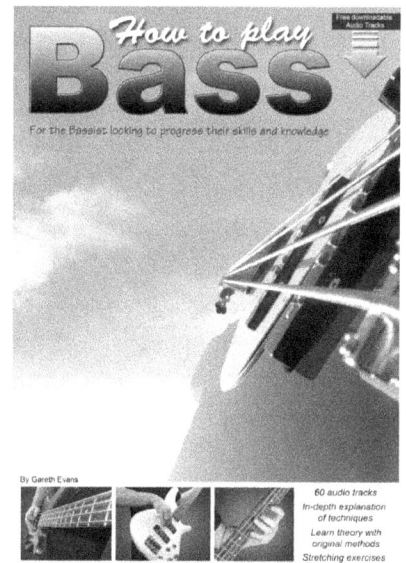

For the bassist looking to progress their skills and knowledge

…and many more!

www.ingramcontent.com/pod-product-compliance
Lightning Source LLC
LaVergne TN
LVHW081449070426
835508LV00016B/1417